World Famous SPY SCANDALS

Vikas Khatri

PUSTAK MAHAL®

Publishers
Pustak Mahal®

J-3/16 , Daryaganj, New Delhi-110002
☎ 23276539, 23272783, 23272784 • *Fax:* 011-23260518
E-mail: info@pustakmahal.com • *Website:* www.pustakmahal.com

Sales Centre

- 10-B, Netaji Subhash Marg, Daryaganj, New Delhi-110002
  ☎ 23268292, 23268293, 23279900 • *Fax:* 011-23280567
  E-mail: rapidexdelhi@indiatimes.com
- **Hind Pustak Bhawan**
  6686, Khari Baoli, Delhi-110006
  ☎ 23944314, 23911979

Branches

Bengaluru: ☎ 080-22234025 • *Telefax:* 080-22240209
E-mail: pustak@airtelmail.in • pustak@sancharnet.in
Mumbai: ☎ 022-22010941, 022-22053387
E-mail: rapidex@bom5.vsnl.net.in
Patna: ☎ 0612-3294193 • *Telefax:* 0612-2302719
E-mail: rapidexptn@rediffmail.com
Hyderabad: *Telefax:* 040-24737290
E-mail: pustakmahalhyd@yahoo.co.in

ISBN 978-81-223-1239-3

Edition: 2011

Printed at : **Param Offsetters, Okhla, New Delhi-110020**

Contents

Introduction

Espionage, the secret collection of information, or intelligence, that the source of such information wishes to protect from disclosure. Intelligence refers to evaluated and processed information needed to make decisions. The term can be used with reference to business, military, economic, or political decisions, but it most commonly relates to governmental foreign and defence policy. Intelligence generally has a national security connotation and therefore exists in an aura of secrecy.

Espionage, or spying, is illegal according to national laws. Spying proceeds against the attempts of counterespionage (or counterintelligence) agencies to protect the secrecy of the information desired.

In the United States, the Central Intelligence Agency, or CIA, is the main agency for gathering secret information that may bear on national security. The Federal Bureau of Investigation, or FBI, has the primary responsibility for counterespionage activities within the U.S., coordinating its work with the CIA, which is responsible for such operations outside the U.S. During the cold war both the FBI and the CIA concentrated their attention primarily on the Komitet gosudarstvennoy bezopasnosti (KGB), or State Security Committee, of the USSR. In the wake of the dissolution of the Soviet Union in 1991 and the breakup of the KGB into several new units, the mission of the CIA came under reexamination by both Congress and the administration. At least initially, the agency remained responsible not only for the collection and analysis of information, but also for counterintelligence overseas and for various forms of covert action (political intervention, secret propaganda, paramilitary activities) that require deep secrecy. Select committees of both the House and the Senate continued their oversight of CIA operations.

International espionage methods and operations have few boundaries. They have been romanticised in popular fiction and the mass media, but in reality, espionage exists in a secret world of deception, fraud, and sometimes violence. Espionage involves the recruiting of agents in foreign nations; efforts to encourage the disloyalty of those possessing significant information; and audio surveillance as well as the use of a full range of modern photographic, sensing, and detection devices, and other techniques of eliciting secret information.

Justification and International Sanction

In order to adopt and implement foreign policy, plan military strategy and organise armed forces, conduct diplomacy, negotiate arms control agreements, or participate in international organisation activities, nations have vast information requirements. Not surprisingly, then, many governments maintain some kind of intelligence capability as a matter of survival in a world where dangers and uncertainties still exist. The cold war may have ended, but hostilities continue in parts of Eastern Europe, the former Soviet Union, the Middle East, and elsewhere.

All nations have laws against espionage, but most sponsor spies in other lands. Because of the clandestine nature of espionage, no reliable count exists of how many Intelligence officers—only a small percentage of whom are actually spies—there are in the world. A common estimate is that the U.S. today still employs some 200,000 intelligence personnel. The number that was generally ascribed to the Soviet intelligence establishment in the 1980s was 400,000, a figure that undoubtedly included border guards and internal security police.

The Gathering of Intelligence

Intelligence work, including spying, proceeds in a five-step process. Initially, what the decision makers need to know is considered, and requirements are set. The second step is collecting the desired information, which requires knowing where the information is located and who can best obtain it. The information may be available in a foreign newspaper, radio broadcast, or other open source; or it may be obtained only by the most sophisticated electronic means, or by planting an agent within the decision-making system of the target area. The third step is intelligence production, in which the collected raw data are assembled, evaluated, and collated into the best possible answer to the question initially asked. The fourth step is communicating the processed information to the decision maker. To be useful, information must be presented in a timely, accurate, and understandable form. The fifth and crucial step is the use of intelligence. The decision maker may choose to ignore the information conveyed, thus possibly courting disaster; on the other hand, a judgement may be made on the basis of information that proves inaccurate. The point is that the decision maker must make the final crucial judgement about whether, or how, to use the information supplied. The intelligence process can fail at each or any of these five basic steps.

A. Recruitment of Agents

Today, scores of developed nations have efficient intelligence organisations with systematic programs for recruiting new agents. Agents come from three main sources: the university world, where students are sought and trained for intelligence careers; the armed services and police forces, where some degree of intelligence proficiency may already have been attained; and the underground world of espionage, which produces an assortment of persons, including criminal informers, with relevant experience.

Those who do the actual spying, which may involve stealing information or performing disloyal acts of disclosure, are led to this work by various motivations. Greed or financial need is a leading incentive in many cases, but other motivations, such as ambition, political ideology, or nationalistic idealism, can figure importantly: Oleg Vladimirovich Penkovsky, a highly placed Soviet officer, provided valuable information to Western intelligence services in the belief that the West must be warned of danger. H. A. R. ("Kim") Philby, the notorious English spy, worked for the Soviet Union on ideological grounds.

Some spies must be carefully recruited and enticed into cooperation; others volunteer and are termed "walk-ins". The latter must be handled with extreme caution, as it is common for double agents to be among the volunteers. Double agents are spies who pretend to be defecting, but in reality maintain their original loyalty. Counterintelligence staffs are always skeptical of walk-ins or defectors and restrict their use for positive espionage purposes. In some cases, the most valuable spy of all is the "agent-in-place", the person who remains in a position of trust with access to highly secret information, but who has been recruited by a foreign intelligence service; such a spy is known as a "mole".

A high-priority espionage target is the penetration of the various international terrorist organisations. If the leadership of such units can be infiltrated by spies, advance knowledge can be obtained of the location and identity of intended victims, the nature of the disguises being used by the hit team, and the secret sources of weapons. Such information could be used to foil terrorist operations. International drug traffic, it has been asserted, can similarly be thwarted by effective espionage, but the problem is complex, and only limited success has been achieved.

B. Espionage Agencies and Networks

The world's intelligence, espionage, counterintelligence, and covert action programs may be said to follow three distinct organisational patterns: the American, the totalitarian (exemplified by the Communist regimes), and the British (parliamentary) systems. Similarities exist among them, yet distinctions are sharp.

In the U.S. the CIA continues to sit at the corner of an elaborate complex of some dozen separate intelligence organisations. Each has a specific role and a carefully guarded area of operations. The director of central intelligence is both head of the CIA and the president's principal intelligence adviser. In the latter job, the director theoretically coordinates all the separate intelligence units, setting their requirements, budgets, and operational assignments. In reality, many of the major units in the system—such as the Defense Intelligence Agency and the huge National Security Agency/ Central Security Service, both part of the Department of Defense—operate in quasi independence. The National Security Agency, which engages in code making and code breaking, is much larger in staff size and budget than the CIA. The military also maintains a major tactical intelligence capability to assist field commanders in making on-the-spot decisions. Other major units in the U.S. intelligence system include the State Department's Bureau of Intelligence and Research, the Department of the Treasury, the FBI, and the Drug Enforcement Administration of the Department of Justice. The U.S. model influenced the intelligence structures of those countries where the U.S. was dominant at the end of World War II, such as West Germany (now part of the united Federal Republic of Germany), Japan, South Korea, and Taiwan.

In contrast to the federated American intelligence structure, the typical totalitarian setup is highly centralised. In the Soviet Union, the power of the KGB pervaded every aspect of national life. Its director was generally a powerful member of the Politburo (the governing political committee of the USSR). The KGB had two chief directorates. The most important was the First Directorate, which was responsible for foreign intelligence gathering. The Second Directorate's principal responsibilities involved providing counterespionage protection to the regime and recruiting foreign agents within the Soviet Union. Its targets included diplomats and journalists stationed in the USSR, foreign students, business persons, tourists, and visiting delegations. Most Eastern European governments followed the KGB model in their intelligence operations. China, Cuba, and other Communist nations still do.

The third model of intelligence systems is the British, a confederation of agencies coordinated by a cabinet subcommittee and accountable to the cabinet and prime minister. The two principal units are the Secret Intelligence Service (often called MI-6, signifying "military intelligence") and the Security Service (popularly called MI-5). These labels reflect the military origins of these services, which are now in the civilian sector. MI-6 is similar to the CIA and the KGB in that it carries out espionage, counterespionage, and covert action overseas. MI-5 is charged with domestic counterintelligence and internal security. Scotland Yard maintains a "special branch", which operates as the overt arm of the security service; it makes arrests and offers evidence in espionage cases while MI-5 agents remain in the background. A number of specialised units also operate within the British intelligence community. These include the Government Communications Centre (for code making and breaking), the Ministry of Defence intelligence sections, and various Foreign Office intelligence groups. With some national variations, the intelligence services of France, Italy, Israel, and the members of the Commonwealth of Nations follow the general British pattern of organisation.

History Of Espionage

Intelligence was early recognised as a vital tool of statecraft—of diplomacy or war. Writing almost 2500 years ago, the Chinese military theorist Sun Tzu (flourished 6th century BC) stressed the importance of intelligence. His book "The Art of War" (circa 500 BC) gave detailed instructions for organising an espionage system that would include double agents and defectors. Intelligence, however, was haphazardly organised by rulers and military chiefs until the rise of nationalism in the 18th century and the growth of standing armies and diplomatic establishments.

A. 19th Century

Political espionage is thought to have first been used systematically by Joseph Fouché, duc d'Otrante, minister of police during the French Revolution and the reign of Napoleon. Under Fouché's direction, a network of police agents and professional spies uncovered conspiracies to seize power organised by the Jacobins and by Bourbon Royalist émigrés. The Austrian statesman Prince von Metternich also established an efficient organisation of political and military spies early in the 19th century.

Better known than either of these organisations was the dreaded Okhrana (Department for Defence of Public Security and Order) of the Russian tsars, created in 1825 to uncover opposition to the regime.

During the mid-19th century, the secret police of Prussia was reorganised and invested with the duty of safeguarding the external as well as the internal security of the country. The Prussian espionage system played an important part in preparations to unify the German states in the German Empire. It also covered France with a network of about 30,000 agents whose work contributed to the German victory in the Franco-Prussian War of 1870-71. Not until the latter part of the 19th century, however, were permanent intelligence bureaus created by modern states.

B. Early 20th Century

Systematic espionage aided the Japanese in defeating the Russians in the Russo-Japanese War of 1904-5. In preparing for World War I, the Germans again flooded France with a host of espionage agents, some of whom were disguised as trade representatives, teachers, agricultural labourers, or domestics. The most famous of the accused agents was Mata Hari, a Javanese dancer in Paris who was eventually executed by the French. German agents also engaged in attempts to sabotage American national defence both before and after the U.S. entry into World War I.

Most nations, however, entered World War I with inadequate espionage staffs, and the war was frequently fought on the basis of poor intelligence. The lessons of that war, along with rapid advances in technology, especially in communications and aviation, spurred a major growth in intelligence agencies. This was further stimulated by the advent of Fascist governments in Europe and a military dictatorship in Japan, all of which had expansionist foreign policies, and the creation of counterespionage agencies such as the Gestapo in Nazi Germany. These developments led other, democratic countries to establish counterespionage systems as well.

C. World War II

World War II was the great stimulus to intelligence services worldwide. Modern military and communications technology put a premium on accurate and quick information, as well as on efforts to protect the security of sensitive information. Some of the great battles of World War II were actually intelligence and counterintelligence battles. Only in recent years have some of the exploits, and failures, in this secret war been disclosed. Notable is Operation Double Cross, in which the British captured practically all the German spies in Britain during the war and turned them into double agents who sent false information back to Germany. Also, the British and their allies were able to break the German secret code, providing access to many of the enemy's secret transmissions.

The surprise attack by Japan on the American naval base at Pearl Harbour on December 7, 1941, was a great intelligence success for the Japanese and an intelligence failure for the Americans. That failure stimulated the postwar growth of a massive intelligence apparatus in the U.S. Before World War II, the U.S. had virtually no intelligence system; after the war the CIA became world famous for its pervasive international surveillance, joining the MI-6, the KGB, the Service de Documentation Extérieure et de Contre-Espionage of France, Israel's foreign intelligence agency, China's Social Affairs Department, and numerous other intelligence agencies in a massive network of espionage and counterespionage efforts.

D. Late 20th Century

In the mid-1970s, as a result of disillusionment with the Vietnam War, the Watergate scandal, and the policies of détente, many Americans began to question the role of the CIA. Mass-media disclosures of intelligence agency abuses and failures were followed by investigations by presidential commissions and congressional committees, which resulted in new guidelines for secret operations and a new structure for executive and legislative supervision. Controversy over the CIA's role and control remains, however. One result is an ever-increasing amount of public information about intelligence services around the world.

E. Espionage in Politics and Industry

Intelligence and espionage are terms most commonly associated with national foreign policies, yet secret information is needed to make decisions in politics, commerce, and industry. Political parties have always been interested in the strategic plans of their opponents or in any information that might discredit them.

Most large corporate enterprises today have divisions for strategic planning that require intelligence reports. Competitive enterprises are undeniably interested in the plans of their competitors; despite laws against such practices, industrial espionage is difficult to detect and control and is known to be an active tool for gaining such foreknowledge. Many of the tools of government intelligence work are used, including electronic surveillance and aerial photographic reconnaissance, and attempts are even made to recruit defectors.

F. Implications of Modern Technology

All forms and techniques of intelligence are now aided by an accelerating technology of communications and a variety of computing and measuring devices. Miniaturised cameras and microfilm have made it easier for persons engaged in all forms of espionage to photograph secret documents and conceal the films. Artificial satellites also have an espionage function—that of aerial photography for such purposes as detecting secret military installations. The vanguard of these developments is highly secret, but it is known that telephones can be tapped without wires, rooms can be bugged (planted with electronic listening and recording devices) without entry, and photographs can be made in the dark. Of course this same technology is used in countermeasures, and the competition escalates between those seeking secret information and those trying to protect it.

In foreign embassies in sensitive areas, confidential discussions routinely take place in plastic bubbles encasing secure rooms, to protect the confidentiality of information. Intelligence agencies have long been known to be staffed with expert lip readers. Privacy of communications remains under constant assault by technological developments that offer threats to, but perhaps also promises for, human progress.

Vernon Kell: Curse of the Kaiser

German agents began infiltrating Britain to prepare for World War I as early as 1902. The authorities took little interest. Then, with the setting up of MO5, later renamed MI5, the police at last found someone who took their espionage warnings seriously. And Vernon Kell, taking on the might of German intelligence single-handedly, realised Scotland Yard's Special Branch men were vital allies. He started close co-operation with Superintendent Patrick Quinn. It paid off just 12 months later.

Kaiser Wilhelm II came to London in 1910 for the funeral of King Edward VII. In his party, there was a naval captain known to be a spymaster. He was trailed to a seedy barber's shop run by Karl Gustav Ernst in the Caledonian Road. It was an unlikely choice for a gentleman who only wanted a haircut. Kell applied for permission to intercept the barber's mail. He discovered that Ernst was Germany's intelligence post-master. Berlin sent him packages containing individual letters of instructions for their agents, to be posted in London. The agents sent back eir reports via Ernst's shop.

Kell and Quinn then played a waiting game. Detectives kept watch on every agent unmasked, but it was vital not to alert them to this fact because the Germans would then replace them, or find new ways of contacting them. It was also important to trace every member of each agent's network. Only when it became obvious that crucial secrets were about to be relayed to Berlin did the counterespionage forces strike. Where possible, information and instructions were merely doctored by the interceptors, sometimes using expert forgers from Parkhurst jail. But some arrests were essential – if there were none, the Germans might smell a rat.

One of Kell's problems was that espionage was not taken seriously by the law. German army lieutenant Siegfried Helm, caught red-handed making detailed sketches of Portsmouth's dockyard defences, was merely bound over to keep the peace and released by a court. Spying in peacetime was not considered an offence.

Kell campaigned for changes in the Official Secrets Act, and in 1911 it was amended to cover collection of information which might be useful to an enemy in future wars. Kell could now prosecute such spies as Dr Armgaard Karl Graves, jailed for 18 months at Edinburgh for snooping on the Navy's Rosyth base and collecting information about weapons from Glasgow companies; Heinrich Grosse, tried at Winchester in 1912 after amassing a huge dossier on ships, submarines and artillery at Portsmouth; and Frederick Adolphus Schroeder, imprisoned for six years in April 1914. As Frederick Gould, he used German intelligence funds to buy the Queen Charlotte public house in Rochester, near the top-secret Chatham dockyard, in 1902. Kell had known about him since 1911, but only pounced when his wife set out by train for Brussels with sensitive data on guns, cruisers and minefields in her bag.

Kell's finest hour came when war was declared on August 4, 1914. Before dawn on the following day, he and the Special

Branch, now led by Sir Basil Thomson, had arrested Ernst the barber – paid £ 1 a month by the Germans – and 23 other spies. Germany's entire intelligence network in Britain were wiped out as agents were seized in London, Newcastle, Barrow in Furness, Portsmouth, Southampton, Brighton, Falmouth and Warwick. German armies battling the French near Mons were amazed to encounter British troops when they tried to outflank their enemy. The British Expeditionary Force had slipped unnoticed across the Channel to the trenches. The furious Kaiser exclaimed: 'Am I surrounded by dolts? Why have I never been told we have no spies in England.' Gustav Steinhauer, who called himself the Kaiser's Master Spy, had no answer.

The Germans tried to form a new network, but with little success. Kell and Thomson supplemented their vigilance with newspaper propaganda campaigns whipping up spy hysteria, and reports of suspect neighbours flooded in. One spy, posing as a Norwegian journalist, was suspected because he was too quiet in his rooms. Detectives discovered invisible ink in a bottle marked gargling lotion.

Two Dutchmen arrived in Portsmouth, posing as cigar salesmen. Their reports to Rotterdam were disguised as orders, 5,000 Coronas representing five warships about to sail. Kell's postal censors were puzzled by the sudden popularity of cigars in Hampshire and detectives were called in. The two spies were arrested and shot. Another agent toured Britain as a music hall trick-cyclist. Censors discovered messages in invisible ink on English song sheets he was sending to Zurich.

Kell made brilliant use of another detected spy. Carl Hans Lody, a German naval reserve officer who had been living in America, landed in Scotland posing as an American tourist in September, 1914. He immediately sent a telegram to his contact in Sweden saying, 'Hope we beat these damned Germans soon.' It was a suspicious communication between representatives of countries supposed to be neutral. Lody was tailed as he travelled round England. The watchdogs could not believe their luck when they discovered he was sending to Germany as fact a British propaganda story stating that Russian troops were landing in Scotland to reinforce the Allies in the European trenches. Lody was later nicknamed the spy who cost Germany the war. Two divisions were withdrawn to watch Channel ports for the Russian arrival, weakening the Kaiser's forces for the vital Battle of the Marne which the Germans might otherwise have won. Lody was eventually arrested and shot at the Tower of London in November 1916.

British intelligence also detected the amorous activities of over-rated sex spy, Mata Hari. Gertrud Margarete Zelle, born in Holland, took the name Mata Hari (it meant Eye of the Morning) when she became an erotic dancer in Paris. During the war, she cashed in on the pleasure sex gave her by sleeping with important military figures on both sides, and selling what they told her to the enemy. In Paris, Berlin and Madrid, she plied her erotic espionage trade, though the secrets she passed were seldom of much value. In 1916, her ship to Holland docked at Falmouth, and she was escorted to London for interrogation. If she persisted in consorting with the Germans, she was warned, she would be in trouble. Mata took no notice. She was later arrested by the French, and shot on 15 October, 1917.

Only one spy escaped the notice of Kell and Thomson – they only learned about him when he wrote his memoirs back in Germany in 1925. Jules Silber could pass as an Englishman after travels in India, America and South Africa. He fought for the British in the Boer Wars, which helped gain him a job in the postal censor's office when he turned up in London in 1914, offering his services. He regularly sent the Kaiser dossiers on what he learned from reading other people's letters. His own mail went undetected because he could stamp it 'passed by the censor'. Silber's most spectacular success was warning Germany about the Q-ships. A girl wrote that her brother was involved in a strange scheme to put guns on old merchant ships. Silber posed as a censor to call on her and warn against future indiscretions. Before he left, she had revealed all he needed to know about the innocent-looking cargo carriers camouflaged to protect Atlantic convoys against German submarine attack.

Silber's information was a rare naval coup for the Kaiser's fleet. For most of the war, British Naval Intelligence under Admiral Sir Reginald Hall – nicknamed Blinker because of a nervous tic in one eye – ruled both the ocean and air waves. Hours after hostilities began, a British ship sliced a hundred yards of cable out of Germany's main under-water telecommunications link with the outside world. This forced the Kaiser's forces to send messages by radio, which could be intercepted at listening stations along the English south coast. The messages were then decyphered in Room 40 of the Admiralty building in London, using naval code books taken during an engagement with the German cruiser Magdeburg on 26 August.

Hall got his hands on the enemy's diplomatic code when a German guerrilla harrying British forces in Turkey fled abandoning his baggage. When a new German transmitter began broadcasts from Brussels, using another code, Naval Intelligence learned that the staff included a British-born cypher clerk called Alexander Szek, who still had relatives living near Croydon in London. Szek agreed to copy the code book, piece by piece. When he completed the task, he vanished. Mystery still surrounds exactly what happened. The British said the Germans discovered his treachery and executed him. French sources claimed that a British agent smuggled

Szek out of Brussels to prevent the Germans to learn their code, then pushed him off ship in the middle of the English Channel to ensure he stayed silent. Another version is that he died in a hit-and-run 'accident' in a Brussels side street. Whatever the cause, Szek's death proved that the British no longer considered espionage a game. It was now a matter of life and death.

Control of the German codes enabled Admiral Sir Reginald Hall to fool the Kaiser with deliberately false messages. In September, 1916, he arranged for one of his agents to leak an emergency code to the Germans, then signalled that ships were sailing from Dover, Harwich and Tilbury with troops to invade the north Belgian coast. To authenticate the information, he had 25 special editions of the Daily Mail newspaper printed, with a spurious story about preparations at 'an East Coast base'. Copies were smuggled to Holland, and passed surreptitiously to German agents. The ploy worked almost too well. The German High Command detached a large force from the trenches and moved it to the coast. But a War Office agent, not told of the subterfuge, warned Whitehall the movement heralded a plan to invade England. The War Office started preparing to evacuate south-east England until it was let in on Hall's secret.

Hall's most significant part in winning the war was the Zimmermann Telegram. The code Szek provided enabled Room 40 decipherers to read a message from the German Secretary of State, Arthur Zimmermann, to his ambassador in Mexico City in January, 1917, warning that unrestricted submarine attacks on neutral Atlantic convoys were about to start, and instructing the envoy to organise Mexican attacks on the southern United States if America entered the war. Hall ensured that the message reached the White House in a way which clearly proved it was not a British invention. Together with the sinking of the liner Lusitania, the telegram forced the United States to abandon its policy of isolation three months later. It was the turning point in Allied fortunes.

Hall, Thomson and Kell had done as much as anyone to earn the victory that finally came on 11 November, 1918. They were abetted by Commander Mansfield Cumming, first chief of the Special Intelligence Section, later MI6, which was founded in 1912 for offensive espionage abroad. One of his agents is said to have alerted Hall's Naval Intelligence to the possibility of using Alexander Szek to obtain the Kaiser's code. His name was Sidney Reilly.

Coomar Narain Episode

John Galbraith, the former American Ambassador in India, once remarked that the bureaucracy in India can be treated as an extension of western espionage network. At that time, this statement seemed to be absurd. When the above episode came to surface, it proved that the assessment of Galbraith was correct to some extent. This is the astonishing story of an espionage ring whose tentacles reached from the office of the President of India to the secretariat of the Prime Minister.

The day was Army day and the date was January 15, 1985. The lawns of the Army Headquarters were crowded by almost all the important personalities in India. The President was there and so was the Prime Minister. Senior members of the Union cabinet rubbed shoulders with high ranking army officers, defence advisors of different Embassies in New Delhi and senior administrative officers of Government of India. The Principal Secretary to the Prime Minister, Dr. P.C. Alexander was engaged in conversation with the Secretary of the Defence Production Department. The military attache of the French Embassy, Col. Alain Bolley was standing nearby.

Also present were a large number of agents of the different intelligence agencies in India. Their eyes were fixed on these people. This was being done for the last two months under a 24 hour surveillance plan. This strict surveillance was rewarded within two days, when the biggest spy scandal in the history of Free India was unravelled and left the entire nation stunned.

During the night of 16th January, the Intelligence Bureau raided the offices of S.L.M. Maneklal situated at 16, Hailey Road. This firm represented many industrial machinery manufacturers of western Europe. It may be mentioned that the firm of S.L.M. Maneklal had prospered at a phenomenal rate during the last few years. Two persons, who were found drinking there, were arrested. One of them was Coomar Narain, a liaison officer of the firm of Maneklal and the other was P. Gopalan, Personal Assistant of the Principal Secretary to the Prime Minister.

Coomar Narain

P.C. Alexander

Immediately after this, the team of detectives arrested Jagdish Chandra Arora from his residence. He had to be awakened from his sleep. Arora was Personal Assistant to the Secretary of the Defence Production Department. The arrests and searches continued for the whole day on 17th January. These operations could be completed only during the night of 17-18 January.

On January 18, 1985, the Prime Minister Rajiv Gandhi reached the Parliament and gave details of this episode to the members of that august body. The Prime Minister was visibly upset but his mood was confident as most of the persons involved in this nefarious activity had been nabbed. He regretted that many persons occupying positions of trust in the government had turned out to be traitors to the motherland.

The military attache of the French Embassy was asked to leave the country. Consultations and analysis started about the foreign involvement in this spy scandal. The administration was really worried about the involvement of so many officers occupying responsible posts in this conspiracy. They were,

T.N. Kher, Personal Secretary to Dr. P.C. Alexander, the Principal Secretary to the Prime Minister, S. Shankaran, Assistant to the Press Secretary of President Zail Singh; two assistants of the Prime Minister's secretariat – A.K. Malhotra and Udai Chand; Jagdish Tewari, who was a senior assistant in the Economic Affairs Department and Jagdish Chandra Arora who was a personal assistant in the office of the Secretary of Defence Production Department.

Kher had been in service for fifteen years and lived in an excellent house in Pamposh colony. Gopalan lived in Ramkrishnapuram. Coomar Narain lived in his own two storeyed house in the posh locality of Defence colony. He also had an agricultural farm in Mehrauli area.

After a thorough investigation, it was confirmed that Coomar Narain was the leader of this gang. He was getting a salary of Rs.7000 per month from his employers but greed for more money led him into spying work. At the time of his arrest in the office at Hailey Road on 16th night, three confidential documents were found in the brief case of Gopalan. These documents were prominently marked 'Secret'. The other documents recovered from Coomar Narain's office in the raid on January 17 are listed below:

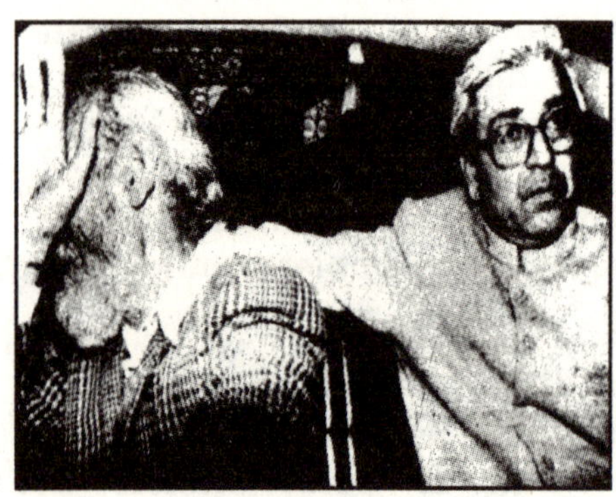

Gopalan (covering face) and Kher

Confidential reports of Intelligence department, Research and Analysis Wing (RAW) and Defence Ministry including 23 bottles of expensive foreign Scotch and Rs. 1,02,890 in cash were found.

A report of the Research and Analysis Wing sent by the Deputy Director of Cabinet Secretariat and addressed to the Principal Secretary of the Prime Minister was found.

Extremely confidential report sent to Principal Secretary, Alexander by Shri R. K. Bhatia, Deputy Director of Intelligence department was found. This report was based on secret information received upto 10th January. It was related to surveillance of the activities of the terrorists.

The report from Intelligence department dated January 15, 1985, containing details of some speeches was also found.

A report regarding Insat satellite sent by Dr. U.R. Rao, Secretary of the Department of Space to the Principal Secretary was discoverd. The original copy of this report was addressed to the Foreign Secretary, Romesh Bhandari. Copy of the letter dated 15.1.85 written by the Defence Ministry to the Defence Production Secretary regarding radars that could be installed at lower heights as also automatic information gathering devices.

The confidential messages sent by Central Code Language Bureau for Foreign Ministry under telex nos. 0317, 00567, 00580, 00577, 00578 and 00584 were found.

A copy of the programme of the Prime Minister for January 17, 1985 was found. It included details about persons meeting him that day. The details of the wealth of Coomar Narain as well as the assessment of the political situation prevailing in the country which was prepared by the Prime Minister's Secretariat were also seized.

The government presented a 2100 page chargesheet and a list of 188 witnesses to the court. It contained a sworn affidavits of persons who affirmed that this gang was active since 1972. Mrs. Gandhi had issued direction in 1982 to keep a strict watch on the Prime Minister's and President's secretariats. The intelligence department knew about this gang from September 1984. They started tightening the noose round the necks of all these people from that time, but the matter was delayed for some time due to the assassination of Mrs. Indira Gandhi on 31st October, 1984.

Traitor on the Queen's Payroll

Anthony Blunt joined Russia's 'Cambridge Circus' of spies even before Donald Maclean. Guy Burgess, himself enlisted by Kim Philby, recruited his fellow homosexual in 1935. But it was before November, 1979, he was publicly unmasked as a traitor by Prime Minister Margaret Thatcher. Though he had confessed to the espionage authorities 15 years earlier, he went unpunished. For the spy who betrayed His Majesty's forces during World War II was, by 1964, Sir Anthony Blunt, Surveyor of the Queen's Pictures. And in 1946, he had spared royal blushes with a delicate, top-secret mission to Germany.

Blunt preceded his fellow Soviet agents to Trinity College, arriving in 1926. The London vicar's son proved such a brilliant scholar that he was offered a teaching post, and was a Fellow of the college when Burgess reached Trinity. The two soon became friends, and Blunt readily agreed to Burgess's suggestion that he work for the Russians to fight the spread of Naziism. When his Soviet spymaster ordered Burgess to London, Blunt took over his task of spotting other talented students likely to join the cause.

By 1939, Blunt too was in London as deputy director of the prestigious Courtauld Institute of Art. When war broke out, he volunteered for military intelligence. He was rejected because of his Marxist past. Astonishingly, he was then accepted by MI5 on the recommendation of an art chum. For the next five years, he undermined the counter-espionage operations of Britain's secret services just as effectively as Kim Philby was wrecking MI6's overseas efforts. Blunt, the spy had caught the spycatchers on the hop.

One of his first acts was to tell Moscow that, for seven years, someone in the office of Politburo member Anastas Mikoyan had been feeding information to MI5. The mole's supply of information stopped immediately. Then Blunt revealed that MI5 had bugged the HQ of the British Communist party. And he kept the Russians informed about the names and duties of every MI5 officer; he was even in charge of the surveillance roster for a time, able to tell Moscow exactly who was watching whom.

Later, Blunt worked closely with Guy Burgess in operations against the neutral embassies in London. Burgess was recruiting Spanish, Portuguese and Scandinavian envoys as agents for MI5. Blunt was involved in the clandestine monitoring of diplomatic pouches and telephone messages. He was thus able to spot likely collaborators for MI5 and the Russians. The two men met regularly in Blunt's rooms at the Courtauld Institute in Portman Square, preparing reports for their Soviet contact and providing secret documents for him to copy. Later in the war, these included plans for Operation Fortitude, a vital propaganda ploy to persuade the Germans that the D-Day landings would be at Pas-de-Calais, not the real target, Normandy. The Russians had an interest in prolonging the war on the Western Front – they could then grab more of Eastern Europe. Fortunately for thousands of Allied lives, they made no use of Blunt's information.

Unusually, the Russians let Blunt leave MI5 at the end of the war. Normally a spy infiltrated into such a useful position would be left in place until discovery loomed, and it was later surmised that Blunt was freed only because there was an equally effective mole in MI5 to provide the service the Kremlin required in the cold war years. But Blunt did not leave the service of Moscow. His new job, as Surveyor of Pictures for King George VI, was perfect cover for his activities as a courier. Nobody would suspect him of running messages for Soviet spies, collecting information and leaving money in secret hiding places for other agents, passing on titbits of information gleaned in casual chats with former MI5 colleagues. Blunt now performed all of these tasks. He became an indispensible back-up to Russia's front line agents. He even saved Philby's skin when Burgess and Maclean fled.

After the diplomats' disappearance in 1951, security forces wanted to inspect Burgess's London flat. Blunt had a key, and let them in. While they searched for incriminating evidence, Blunt noticed three letters implicating both Burgess and Philby in traitorous activities. He quietly pocketed them.

The Russians knew Blunt would be questioned after the disappearance of his former colleague Burgess, and they told him to defect. Blunt, delighted with his new post and prestige as Buckingham Palace adviser, declined, saying he was confident of surviving any interrogation. Again, the Russians let him have his way. And despite 11 MI5 grillings over the next 12 years, he lived up to his promise. He was even able to continue to run messages for the Soviets, helping to reactivate Philby in 1954, and visiting him in Beirut.

Then, in 1963, his luck ran out. A brilliant young American recruited by Moscow at Cambridge in the 1930s was offered an art consultancy job in Washington by President Kennedy. Though he turned it down, he took the opportunity to clear his conscience. He admitted providing the Russians with personal appraisals of American attitudes, and named Blunt as the 'known Soviet agent' who had enlisted him and others.

In April, 1964, Blunt was confronted with his information by MI5 interrogator Arthur Martin. Then he was told that the Attorney General Sir John Hobson, had authorised his immunity from prosecution if he confessed.

Without knowing what Blunt had done, and forgetting the Attorney General's rider – immunity from prosecution only if he had stopped spying in 1945 when Russia was still an ally – MI5 had wiped Blunt's slate clean. Now he was able to confess, which he did, and name some people he had recruited. He was also able to give misleading information to protect others.

Why was immunity so readily given? It is true MI5 had no hard evidence on which to base a successful prosecution, and could justify allowing one spy off the hook if he led them to more. But no one at that stage knew the enormity of Blunt's crimes which, if detected in war time, would have sent him to the gallows for treason. The real reason for the unpublished 'pardon' was Blunt's royal connections.

In 1946, Buckingham Palace asked MI5 to nominate a trustworthy volunteer for a delicate mission in Germany. Blunt was no longer on the secret service staff, but agreed to undertake the task. He never revealed what it entailed, but the following year, having accomplished it, he was presented with the Commander of the Royal Victorian Order award. The mission may also have been a factor in his knighthood, awarded in May, 1956. In January 1983, Chapman Pincher reported in the Daily Express that MI5 officers believed the task was to retrieve records of possibly embarrassing conversations between Hitler and the Duke of Windsor – the present Queen's uncle – during the Duke's visits to Berlin in 1937. Blunt next day denied the report, claiming, rather implausibly, that he merely collected letters Queen Victoria wrote to her daughter, Empress Frederick of Prussia. He did not explain why it was so vital to collect them so soon after the war, half a century after they were written.

Clearly, dragging the Royal Family into a spy trial in the early 1960s, when there were more than enough spy trials anyway, was not in anyone's interests. So while less significant Soviet agents like Vassall began 18 year jail sentences, Blunt retained his Palace job, his prestige and his reputation until, in 1978, author Andrew Boyle published his book, The Climate of Treason. Blunt was not named, but his exploits were. And public opinion was so outraged at the new revelations in the Burgess, Maclean, Philby saga that Mrs. Thatcher was forced to act and Blunt was finally, publicly unmasked. He died in March 1983, aged 76, unloved and unmourned, stripped off his titles and totally disgraced.

Blunt gave interrogators many names of other Russian agents, mainly minor and no longer operating, but he always denied there was a so-called Fifth Man in the 'Cambridge Circus'. According to Chapman Pincher, the security authorities know there was – and know who he was. In his book, Their Trade Is Treachery, he reveals that the spy was recruited by Burgess and Philby in Cambridge after Philby returned from Vienna, that he hid his Communist convictions to gain work at a government defence station as a scientific civil servant, and that he knew two top Russian controllers, Yuri Modin and Sergei Kondrashev, who was sent to Britain specifically to handle the scientist and George Blake.

In 1966, when confronted with evidence about his Communist past and offered immunity from prosecution, he declined to confess. As he was near retirement, he was allowed to qualify for his pension on non-secret work. Exactly who he was, and the damage he did, will have to wait, according to Pincher, until death renders the libel laws irrelevant.

Oil Salesman Extraordinary

American spies monitoring German manoeuvres before the decisive Battle of the Rhine in 1945 stared in astonishment as Hitler's on-the-run army prepared for its last stand. Horses were pulling ammunition trucks to the front and tanks were being dragged into position by oxen. It was final proof of the success of one of the most dangerous espionage exploits of the war. Businessman Eric Erickson had fooled the Nazi top brass for more than three years. Travelling freely through Germany, once on a pass personally provided by SS supremo Heinrich Himmler, he located and inspected vital oil and synthetic fuel refineries, then told Allied bombers the best way to destroy them. But his triumph was achieved at a tragic price. To maintain his cover, Erickson was forced to watch helplessly as a firing squad slaughtered the girl he loved.

Erickson, born in Brooklyn, New York, had become an international oil dealer and a Swedish citizen by the time war broke out. During his worldwide travels, he was often in Germany and had noticed with concern the rise of the Nazis. Then, over dinner in Stockholm with an old acquaintance, Laurence Steinhardt, the American ambassador to Russia, he was offered a way of hitting back. Steinhardt knew that, sooner or later, America would become embroiled in the fighting. Already its secret services were preparing for the day. But they needed information on the Nazi oil supply lifelines. Erickson, with fluent German, established contacts in the Reich and good reasons for going there on business, could provide it. Would he? Erickson quickly agreed to try.

For eighteen frustrating months, he carefully cultivated a new image. He alienated all his old friends by angrily denouncing their anti-Nazi opinions, often in public. He hung pictures of Hitler in his office and home. Gradually, he built up contacts at the German Legation. As a final coup de grace, he persuaded Prince Carl Gustav Bernadotte, nephew of King Gustav, to forfeit popularity in neutral Sweden by pretending to sympathise with the Nazis. The Prince, convinced that Erickson's mission might shorten the war, bravely agreed to dine with local German big-wigs and flatter their snobbish egos. In September 1941, Erickson was at last allowed a visa for a business trip to Germany, having overcome all distrust at his American origins. Only one other Swede knew he was playing a role – his new bride, Ingrid.

The Gestapo were waiting when his plane touched down at Berlin's Tempelhof airport, and Obersturmbannfuhrer Baron Franz von Nordhoff gave him a severe grilling about his attitudes to Hitler, the Nazis, America and the possibility of a Nazified Sweden. The smooth-tongued spy eased his way out of every tight corner, and was allowed to continue with his tour, ostensibly to buy German oil for his country. He memorised everything that might prove useful to the

Allies. He also recruited a network of twelve trusted old friends to provide him with information about the oil plants where they worked. It took time to convince them that he was really working for the Americans, and was not a Nazi agent provocateur. Many demanded a slip of paper, signed by Erickson, to prove to the Allies after the war that they had helped the cause. Erickson knew that each document would be his death warrant if it fell into German hands, but he had no choice but to sign.

Erickson travelled from Berlin to Hamburg, and on to Halle and Hanover. He memorised the exact layout of refineries, production details, nearby landmarks, the site of anti-aircraft batteries and fighter plane airfields. And on his return to Sweden, he poured the detailed data into a Dictaphone tube provided by American agents. Soon the oil Erickson had bought in exchange for iron ore credits began to arrive. Unknown to the Nazis, some of it was used to fuel British patrol boats which were running the German naval blockade of Scandinavia to collect Swedish ball-bearings and other precious parts needed in the war effort.

When the Japanese attack on Pearl Harbour brought America into the war officially, Erickson came under more severe pressure. Some of his relations in the US cut all connections with the 'Nazi-lover'. The Gestapo checked him out again, even taking the trouble to collect his records from Cornell University where he had taken an engineering degree in 1921. Once more he was able to set their minds at rest, and throughout 1942 he made several trips to Germany, sometimes with Prince Carl. He also began visiting countries under Nazi occupation, inspecting refineries commandeered for the Reich war effort. On 12 June, his information was acted on for the first time. American B-24 bombers flew from Egypt to attack the vital oil base at Ploesti, Rumania. Thereafter the businessman-spy spent hours in air raid shelters during his trips to Germany as the US Eighth Air Force accurately blasted refineries in Hamburg, Hanover, Marienburg and Ludwigshafen. During the summer of 1943,

177 heavy bombers attacked Ploesti again. Erickson and his network were able to report that they had knocked out more than 40 per cent of the plant's refining capacity.

Erickson was living on a knife-edge. Apart from the possibility of being killed by the planes his intelligence was guiding, there was the constant fear of betrayal to the Gestapo, either by one of his agents or by accident. A crisis blew up when Hamburg contact Otto Holtz, one of the men who demanded a potentially lethal slip of paper, died unexpectedly. Erickson had to fly to Germany and retrieve the evidence from the bank vault before the man's pro-Nazi widow or son found it. It took two nerve-racking days of tact and subterfuge.

There was little escape from the relentless pressure. Erickson dared not let himself relax for a moment. When forced to share rooms at crowded hotels with other travellers, he took pills to stay awake, afraid of giving himself away by talking in his sleep. Then, late in 1942, he met attractive brunette Marianne von Mollendorf, another secret Allied agent. He became a courier to smuggle her secrets out of Germany, and she advised him on oil contacts and political changes. At first they pretended to be lovers to cover the clandestine meetings. Later, they no longer needed to pretend.

In May 1944, waves of Allied bombers began blitzing refineries throughout the Reich. German fighters sent up to fend them off were ruthlessly shot down, 2,500 in one month alone. As the Luftwaffe ran short of planes, Nazi oil production was cut by half and more than 100,000 men diverted to repair work. The damage was a significant factor in the success of the D-Day landings and the long haul to Berlin. But it also gave Erickson a problem. The Germans now had no surplus oil to sell to Sweden. The excuse for his business trips had vanished. Then he came up with a brilliant solution. Instead of buying oil, he would pose as a seller. He offered to build a synthetic fuel refinery in Sweden, safe from the bombers, to supply the creaking Nazi war machine.

German officials in Stockholm were impressed by the carefully forged dossier of plans and bogus pledges of financial backing from influential Swedes. They forwarded them to Berlin, and Erickson followed to wine and dine decision makers. It took time to convince them, and required several trips to the German capital. Late in 1944, he flew into Templehof again – and was whisked off to the worst moment of his life.

Gestapo men, waiting as usual, drove him away, but not to their massive grey HQ at 8 Prinz Albrechtstrasse. This time the destination was Moabat jail. Erickson was convinced that his espionage had been discovered, and he knew, from past the warnings, how the Nazis dealt with those who betrayed their trust. Gloomily, he watched from a cell window as a guard loaded a machine gun in the prison courtyard. Then he was led out into the sunshine. With relief he saw, he was just one of a group of foreign visitors privileged to witness some executions. But when the condemned prisoners were led out, his heart turned to stone. Among them was Marianne van Mollendorf.

Fury and fear fought within him. Did the Nazis know of their liaison? Would Marianne think he had betrayed her? Could he, even at this late stage, do anything to save her? Was this all a charade to trap him into incriminating action? Their eyes met, but Marianne showed no flicker of recognition. Erickson steeled himself, battling for self-control, as she stood proudly in line. He forced himself to watch as the machine gun cut her and the other prisoners to ribbons.

Erickson went through the motions in the days that followed. And before the end of the week, he was granted an interview about the proposed Swedish refinery by SS chief Himmler himself. It was soon clear that the Reichfuhrer was as mentally unstable as rumours suggested, but Erickson cautiously managed to persuade him of the need for a personal inspection of German synthetic fuel plants to establish exactly what would be required in Stockholm. He was given a pass which allowed unrestricted travel.

Erickson began his tour, but was quickly aware, despite Himmler's words, that the Gestapo were tailing him. It was important to let them do so. As a businessman, he was not supposed to know about espionage techniques, but it meant adapting rendezvous tactics. Information had to be left in the form of seemingly innocent notes on restaurant tables, slipped to contacts at fleeting meetings on street corners, whispered in the darkened corridors of bordellos. Finally, in Leipzig, Erickson's luck ran out. He was recognised by Franz Schroeder, an ardent Nazi who remembered the Swede's pre-war, pro Jewish attitude. Erickson took him for beers at a tavern to try to explain his change of heart, but he could see Schroeder was unimpressed. When they parted, Erickson knew the German would alert the Gestapo. He had to be silenced. But first, the spy had to shake off his SS shadow.

Darting through a nearby hotel, he leapt into a taxi, flashed his authority from the Gestapo chief, and ordered the driver to take the road down which Schroeder had walked. He soon spotted his quarry, and paid off the taxi to follow on foot. Schroeder went into a telephone box, and Erickson crept closer. Sure enough, the German was phoning an SS friend about his suspicions. Before he could go into details, Erickson pounced, driving his pocket knife into the back of the man's head, and wresting the phone from him. Memories of Marianne's death flashed through his mind, strengthening his resolve, somehow hardening his heart against natural repugnance at killing for the first time. As the body slumped to the floor of the kiosk, Erickson vanished into the shadows.

Convinced that it would not take his Gestapo shadow long to make a connection between the body and the man Erickson had met, the Swede cabled Prince Carl, using the code which signified an emergency. By return came a telegram saying Erickson's wife was seriously ill, and he should come to Stockholm immediately. Sending his apologies to Himmler, who was due to meet him again, Erickson took the first available flight out of Germany. His American controllers agreed he could risk no more trips. But already he had done enough.

Bombing raids continued to sap the strength of Hitler's forces. Now the chemical plants Erickson reconnoitred were targets. The Nazis retreated through Europe, abandoning tanks, trucks and jeeps to conserve fuel. The Luftwaffe cut back on training time for pilots and tests on aircraft engines for the same reason, with catastrophic results. And munitions factories using the by-products of the synthetic fuel process ran short of raw material for shells and bombs.

In Stockholm, Erickson and Ingrid devoured every report of Allied advances, and rejoiced on 7 May, 1945 at the German surrender. But they remained outcasts for another month. Then the cream of Swedish society were invited to a party at the American embassy. As they sipped their cocktails, the guests of honour were announced – and in walked the Ericksons and Prince Carl. Gasps of shocked disgust soon turned to humble apologies as the truth behind their pro-Nazi stance was at last revealed. And within days, newspapers throughout the world were hailing the secret heroes who had done so much to crush Hitler.

The Scandal of Larkins Brothers

If Coomar Narain gang carried on its spying activities with the help of government servants, this was a spying scandal of greater magnitude as high ranking armed forces officers were its main characters. Who could imagine that a retired Air Vice Marshal of the Indian Air Force and another retired Major General of the army were carrying on the business of selling defence secret? To top it all they were brothers. They got easy access to every place and could garner information with ease because of the high positions they held in the armed forces. There seemed no way to stop them, but then like most spying scandals, it ended in their exposure and conviction.

The orderly picked up the phone at the residence of Group Captain Jasjit Singh and enquired, "Who is it, Sir."

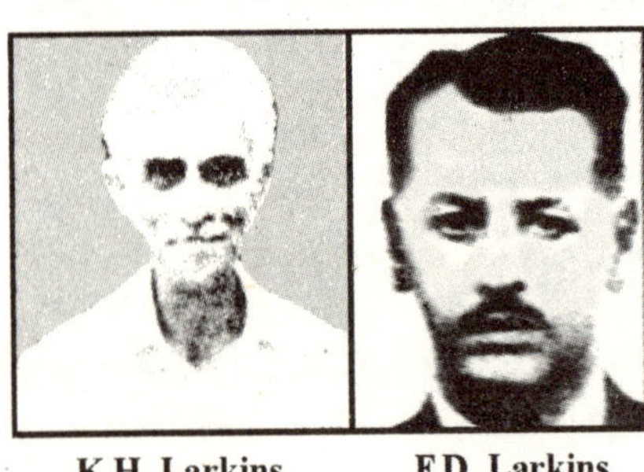

K.H. Larkins F.D. Larkins

He stiffened and stood at attention as the caller identified himself. Group captain who happened to pass that way, took over the phone. It was Air Vice Marshall K.H. Larkins who had called. After the initial greetings and pleasantries, Larkins said, "It is well nigh impossible to meet you. I had been to the Air Headquarters to see you. Singh, why don't you lunch with me at the Ashoka Hotel today."

Group Captain Singh somehow wanted to avoid him. He replied, "Not today Sir, I would be awfully busy today." But, Larkins was not a man who could take 'no' as an answer. "You must be free tomorrow. We can keep the appointment for tomorrow. I hope it suits you," pleaded the man on the other side.

Group Captain Singh had to say 'yes'. He had lived in the disciplined atmosphere of the army for long. There, a senior is a senior and his desires are looked upon as commands. Singh had served under Larkins as a Squadron Leader in 1968. Next day, Singh reached Ashoka Hotel to keep his lunch appointment. The date was March 23, 1983.

This lunch proved expensive for Air Vice Marshal Larkins. It led to exposure of his spying activities as Group Captain Singh did not bite the bait. After drinks and lunch, Larkins broached the subject. He handed over a list to Group Captain Singh and told him that if he could get him those documents he would be paid Rs.20,000 per The next morning, Group Captain Singh made it a point to inform Air Vice Marshal S. Raghvendra at the earliest opportunity regarding his lunch meeting with Larkings. The Air Vice Marshal was stunned. He could not imagine that an officer who had held such a high rank in the Air Force and was known for his valour had sunk so low.

The matter was discussed amongst top officers. Officers from the intelligence branch were also consulted. Eventually, it was decided to hand over a document to Larkins. The idea was to find out his contacts and nab them in one sweep. Hence, a Manual listed in the paper, which contained details regarding oxygen tanks in the planes, directions and charts was handed over to Larkins. On April 4, Air Vice Marshal Larkins drove to the residence of Group Captain Singh and returned the Manual with Rs.10,000 in fifty rupee notes. He informed Singh that if he did his bidding, he could earn a lot of money.

Larkins was totally unaware that officers of Intelligence Bureau and Research and Analysis Wing (RAW) were keeping an eye on his movements. He proceeded to his elder brother's house. His brother F.D. Larkins was seen going to a branch of Syndicate Bank situated at Shakuntala Apartments. The same day, at 4.45 p.m., Larkins was observed going towards Palam airport on Gurgaon Road with a brief case by members of Military Intelligence and detectives of RAW. The

Major-General stopped his car near some vacant plots at Subroto Park. He got down from the car and seemed to be waiting for someone. Soon a car approached him from the opposite direction and a foreigner got down. Major General Larkins handed him a packet. At 7.25 p.m., Major General Larkins met the same foreigner. This time the foreigner gave a packet to F.D. Larkins. In this way, the detectives kept an eye on these spies for nearly nine months. The phones of both the brothers were tapped. Details regarding persons whom they met were meticulously maintained. These people were also photographed with the help of infra-red cameras capable of taking photographs from long distances and even in dark.

In the mean time, the Larkins brothers got the wind of what was happening or somebody alerted them that soon they were going to be arrested. The two officers of the American Embassy, whom they met frequently were sent out of India. These officers were — Albert A. Thibault and Paul Kinley Pittman alias Bud. The brothers decided to emigrate to Australia to escape the noose tightening round their necks. But, they were put under arrest on September 10, when they were both celebrating the birthday of their wives.

A lot of secret documents were seized from the house of Major General Larkins together with an unlicensed gun and bottles of foreign liquor. A case under the Official Secrets Act and Arms Act was filed against him. He was also charged under Excise Act. After some time, he expressed a desire to become an approver in the case and gave a confessional statement. He told the court that he was passing defence secrets to four American agents with his brother K.H. Larkins. Another accomplice was Lt. Col. Jasbir Singh Gill. He disclosed the names of the four American agents as Jockey, John, Ben and Bud. He testified that America wanted the information regarding the next Army Chief. They wanted to know if Srinagar-Leh road was patrolled at night. America also required the names of officers who were being trained outside India in the use of arms and equipment being supplied by foreign countries. They also required information about Russian instructors training Indian officers and where they were posted. He was offered Rs.30,000 for all this information, by agent Jockey.

The packet given to the foreigner on April 4 by Larkins contained instructions, technical details and diagrams of spare parts of the Russian plane MIG-21. He was returned the original documents with a payment of Rs.20,000. For getting the required information asked for by the Americans, Air Vice Marshal Larkins visited Air Headquarters at least 90 times, as was evident from the entry register of that place.

Lt. Col. Jasbir Singh was working with these brothers and was getting only Rs. 1,000 for a document. He had started work in 1980 and gathered information on Russian equipment, T-72 Russian tanks and other sensitive matters. He got help from many officers. After his retirement from the army, Jasbir Singh was in the employ of one Jaspal Singh Gill. Gill was also an American spy. A large amount of confidential and important documents were recovered from his place.

Deadly Deceptions of a Double Agent

The British public was stunned in May, 1961 when it was announced that a spy called George Blake had been jailed for 42 years. It was an astonishing long sentence compared to those imposed on Nunn May, Fuchs and the Portland spy ring. What had Blake done? The trial had been held in secret, in the interests of 'national security', and Prime Minister Harold Macmillan refused to divulge the facts of the case despite repeated attempts by the Labour opposition to raise the matter in Parliament. Eventually, he agreed to a confidential briefing for three Labour Privy Councillors so that minds could be put at rest. But what he told them had the opposite effect.

Blake was born in Rotterdam in 1922, the son of Albert William Behar, an Egyptian Jew who held a British passport, and his Dutch wife. The teenager George Behar joined the Dutch Resistance to Nazi occupation, but was eventually forced to flee to Britain, where he enrolled in secret organisations to carry on the war against Germany, finally changing his name to Blake, and working as an intelligence officer with the Royal Navy Volunteer Reserve.

After the war he was transferred to the Foreign Office, where his brilliance as a linguist was quickly recognised. The Fuchs case brought in new rules, insisting that all civil servants should be British born, but by then Blake was already in the fold, working as a vice consul – and MI6 agent – in Korea. He was captured by the Communists and held in a North Korean interrogation camp for some months. Later suggestions that he was brainwashed at this stage were contradicted by fellow prisoners, who said Blake stood up bravely to his jailers.

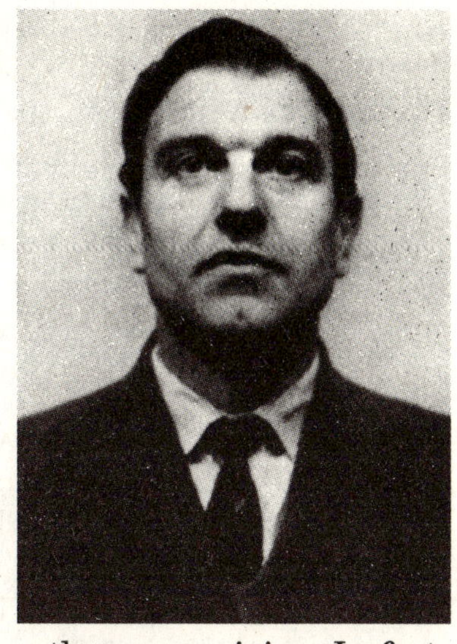

By 1953, he was in Berlin for MI6, with instructions to infiltrate the Soviet spy set-up in the city that was, throughout the 1950s, the frontline flashpoint of the cold war between East and West. For more than four years, London was satisfied with his work in the complex, confused, murky waters of double agent espionage. Naturally, to win the trust of the Russians, he had to provide certain secrets, but MI6 remained confident that they were getting more than they were giving. In fact, they were being duped.

In 1961, the arrest of a German spy and the defection of a Pole both provided evidence, too late, that Blake had turned triple agent. The spy was then based in Beirut. Interception of his message to Moscow, warning that Gordon Lonsdale was about to be arrested, was the final proof MI6 needed. An agent was sent to Lebanon to discuss a new job for Blake in London. It was the technique used with Kim Philby two years later. Philby fled to Russia. Blake, presumably unaware that he had been unmasked, returned to England – and was arrested.

The Macmillan government tried to justify the secret trial on the grounds that agents betrayed by Blake were still being withdrawn from behind the Iron Curtain. In fact, by then, they had all been rounded up and either shot or imprisoned. More than 40 anti-Communist agents around the world had been compromised. There were more secret shocks in store for the Labour Privy Councillors – leader Hugh Gaitskell, deputy leader George Brown and ex-minister Emanuel 'Manny' Shinwell – as they were briefed by Mr Macmillan and his Cabinet Secretary Norman Brook.

In Berlin, Blake had photographed almost every secret document that crossed his desk and handed the snaps to the KGB. He had hidden in the office when it was locked by a security man for the lunch hour, and worked undisturbed. He had informed the Russians of the whereabouts of prominent East Germans who had defected to the West, allowing the KGB to kidnap them and whisk them back behind the Iron Curtain. And he had betrayed one of the West's most expensive and ambitious projects, Operation Gold.

This was a joint project between the CIA and MI6 to build a tunnel to tap East German and Russian messages in East Berlin. It was conceived in December, 1953 and took three months to dig. It began on the site of a new radar station near a cemetery at Rudow, in the Western sector of Berlin, and stretched nearly 0.8 km (1/2 mile) under the barbed wire of the border, 7.3 m (24ft) below street level.

Huge iron pipes, 2.1 m (7 ft) in diameter, linked large chambers containing monitoring equipment, a telephone exchange switchboard and an air-conditioning plant. Highly sophisticated microphones, amplifiers, tape-recorders, teleprinters and transformers made it possible for the American, British and German eavesdroppers to listen to 400 conversations at any one time. Lines were tapped from East German government offices, the KGB HQ in Karlshorst and the Soviet Army command post, with links to Moscow and other Warsaw Pact capitals.

During the first winter, heat rising from the tunnel began to melt snow on the ground above. A refrigeration system was quickly installed along the ceiling, and work on de-coding messages carried on inside the electrically-sealed security doors of the clandestine chambers.

Then, on 22 April 1956, East German border guards and Soviet intelligence staff began digging above the eastern end of the tunnel. Alarms gave the eavesdroppers time to escape, but the Western secret services had to watch mortified as the Russians milked every ounce of propaganda out of their 'discovery', giving guided tours to an estimated 40,000 people.

In fact, the CIA had suspected for some months that the tunnel had been detected. Telecommunications traffic from the tapped offices had dropped dramatically. Their suspicions were confirmed after Blake's arrest. He later claimed that he told Moscow about the project as soon as it was given the go-ahead. Had the West been deliberately misled for nearly three years?

Blake's treason continued in the Middle East. In 1958, the Egyptians exposed the entire British spy network in the area. Some agents were arrested. Others under diplomatic cover in embassies had to be hurriedly withdrawn, and President Nasser threatened to name every spy over Cairo Radio. He never did, but it took years for a replacement network to be set up.

Nasser had no reason to love the British. Two years earlier, Prime Minister Anthony Eden had sent troops ashore in the Suez crisis, and there are suspicions that MI6 was involved at the time in a plot by Egyptian rebels to assassinate their leader – a plot that was never put into action. But the reason for the 1958 clear-out was not primarily revenge. The Kremlin was about to supply Nasser with arms, and did not want British spies around to report the fact. Thanks to Blake, they were not.

Were Blake's superiors at fault, allowing him to know too much? Critics of MI6, while acknowledging that a double agent has to sacrifice some secrets, say that to feed him too many vital ones makes him vulnerable to blackmail or torture if captured – and the spymasters culpable if he proves a traitor. Colonel Charles Gilson, head of the Russian section of MI6 on the Continent until about 1958, shot himself in Rome after retiring. Money problems were the official reason.

Blake, who was second only to Kim Philby as M16's most damaging traitor, served just a fraction of his 42 year sentence. On 22 October 1967, he kicked out a weakly-cemented window bar at Wornwood Scrubs Prison, London, and vanished, resurfacing soon afterwards in Moscow. Once again, the KGB had looked after one of their own – and he had had time to write an ironic farewell. It was Blake's job to look after administration in the prison canteen. One the day of his escape, he had entered all the expenses and income in the accounts ledger, then added a note of apology – he had not had time to add up the totals.

Lonley Hearts and Ruthless Ravens

A flock of ravens proved in March, 1979, that beautiful female swallows are not the only agents to come from Russia with love. Ravens was the nickname given to handsome, smooth-talking Casanova comrades who moved into Western Europe's administrative capitals in force to seduce lonely secretaries. Once the love-hungry girls were hooked, NATO's most sensitive secrets were Moscow's for the taking. And they were taken in their hundreds. Only when four secretaries fled to East Germany in one week was the scope of the problem realised. Yet the espionage exploits of reds in the beds were no new phenomenon.

It was the summer of 1960 when Leonore Heinz cautiously opened the front door of her Bonn apartment. There stood Heinz Suetterlin, nervously fiddling with a bunch of red roses. He explained that he had been given the address after answering an advertisement in a newspaper 'lonely hearts' column, but now he could see there had been some terrible mistake. Leonore, 35 and frightened of being left on the marital shelf, was intrigued by the flattery, and invited the charming caller in for coffee. In fact there had been no mistake. Lonely Leonore was the carefully-selected target for a ruthless romantic assault.

Suetterlin had been meticulously coached for the task. He had learned how to live in the West at specially created camps in Russia. Whole towns, complete with shops, cinemas and restaurants, have been built there to simulate major cities in Britain, America, Germany and Japan. Spies live there for months, familiarising themselves with their future environments by speaking only the language of their eventual destination, learning all about its currency and way of life.

As a raven, Suetterlin was then trained in every trick of seduction and making love. Nubile Soviet girls act as sex tutors; during lessons which, according to one 1960s defector, are 'designed to turn us into animals capable of satisfying the cravings of any woman'. The defector said the pressure on the Red Romeos was so intense that two of his classmates committed suicide. But Suetterlin was made of sterner stuff.

Over coffee, he used every ounce of his practised charm on Leonore. She was amazed to find how much they had in common. They talked all evening, and made a date for dinner the next night. Concerts and romantic walks along the banks of the Rhine followed. Soon Leonore was hopelessly in love with Suetterlin. He was gentle, considerate and generous, in bed and out of it. Within six months they agreed to marry. Leonore was the envy of all her colleagues in the West German government's Foreign Ministry.

But the honeymoon was soon over. Weeks after their wedding, Suetterlin asked his bride to bring home classified documents from the office. Fear of losing the man she had waited for so long persuaded Leonore to do as he wished. She was given a handbag with a false compartment into which she put the papers just before going home to lunch. While she cooked their meal, Suetterlin photographed the secrets, which were returned to the Foreign Ministry during the afternoon. The

Kremlin left instructions and picked up undeveloped rolls of film from hidden 'dead letter box' hiding places in derelict buildings or tree stumps. Suetterlin was alerted to each delivery when a tango titled 'Moscow Nights' was played on Radio Moscow.

In six years, more than 3,000 highly-classified documents found their way to KGB headquarters. They included full details of two vital NATO exercises to test the combat-readiness of West Germany's front-line forces, minutes of crucial NATO conferences and warnings of counter-intelligence operations against Iron Curtain espionage agents. Secret missile centres and evacuation plans in the event of a Russian invasion were also betrayed to Moscow. And the Suetterlin-Leonore service was so efficient that KGB chiefs began to suspect it. Surely, they reasoned, no security service could be lax enough to allow leaks on this scale. But it was.

The Suetterlin operation came to an end in 1967 only because Yevgeny Runge, his spymaster, defected to the West, giving full details of that and other espionage coups. He told West German interrogators:

'The Suetterlins copied the personal files of diplomats and functionaries of the foreign service. These provided an ideal starting point for further entrapments or blackmail. Thanks to Lola (Leonore's KGB code name), we knew well ahead of time whenever an investigation had been ordered against any of our agents. We received copies of all Foreign Ministry messages which had to pass across Lola's desk on their way to the coding room. Often we read them in Moscow before the German Foreign Minister got a chance to read them in Bonn!'

The couple were arrested, but at first Leonore refused to say anything to incriminate her husband. Then she was shown his statement. She was only one of three women he had been sent to Germany to woo. He never loved or, even liked her. Their meeting, courtship and marriage was all ordered by

Moscow. During sex, his passion was always merely duty. Leonore said nothing as she read the harsh words. But that night she hanged herself in her cell with the cord from her dressing gown. Suetterlin was jailed for seven years.

Leonore Heinz was a tragic victim of the Bonn syndrome exploited so ruthlessly by Moscow. The artificially-created nerve centre of the West German and NATO administrations sucks in tens of thousands of ambitious girls as secretaries, receptionists, clerical assistants and switchboard operators. They have lavish apartments, responsible jobs, stylish cars

and plenty of money. Only one thing is lacking – men. The bureaucrats they work with are mostly married and available only for short-term casual affairs. The nightlife is nowhere near as sophisticated as that of Paris, London or New York. The frustrated spinsters are vulnerable to any man who offers availability and diversion. And in the late 1970s, there were suddenly scores of such men.

Helga Berger was 38, a secretary in the Foreign Ministry where Leonore had worked, when a stranger approached as she sat at a cafe beside the Rhine. Peter Krause, fortyish and well-dressed, soon swept her off her feet with expensive dinners, and nights at the opera, cinema and theatre. They became lovers and went on holiday together in Spain. Then came the catch. Krause said he worked for British intelligence, and introduced her to a man claiming to be the head of the UK secret service. There seemed no harm in obtaining classified papers for the agent of a NATO ally. Months later, Krause revealed the truth – he was an East German spy. By then, it was too late for Helga. For years she continued to provide him with information. 'I did not want to lose him,' she tearfully said at her trial. 'I loved him, loved him.' When she began a five-year jail sentence, Krause was back in East Germany.

Dagmar Scheffler was also left to pick up the pieces after being loved and deserted. Dagmar, 35, who worked in the personal office of the West German Chancellor, had just been divorced when smooth-talking Herbert Schroeter walked into her life. Soon she was providing him with details of West Germany's defence policy, the West's position on Soviet neglect of human rights and Bonn's attitude towards Moscow. Schroeter was warned in time to flee to Russia just before Dagmar was arrested. 'I needed a man and Herbert was my dream,' she said. 'I was besotted.'

Renate Lutze, 39, was another secretary duped by a raven. She passed more than 1,000 sensitive documents from her office – that of a top West German defence official – to the man who wooed and wed her during a six year espionage spree before they both were arrested.

Then, in March 1979, came the devastating defection of at least six secretaries in one month. Four fled across the Berlin Wall in one week. The six included Christel Broszey, 32-year-old chief secretary to the leader of the West German opposition, Inge Goliath, 35, secretary to the party's foreign affairs spokesman, Ingeborg Schultz, 36, from the Science Ministry, and Belga Roedinger, 44, who worked in the Finance Ministry.

A NATO spokesman said, 'With every girl who has defected, we have found there was a Communist agent lover. When a girl has fallen for him, it is almost impossible for her to escape. She has found an attentive lover who is superb in bed because he has been trained to be.' West German counter intelligence chief Herbert Hellenbroich said:

'These are older women who have achieved a position of trust and reliability by devoting themselves to their careers, then found they have nothing in their personal lives. They can easily be led into love, and Communist agents can even reveal their identity without the risk of being exposed. The woman will be dependent on them for love, terrified of losing the man who has brought romance into her life.'

But the raven problem was not unique to Germany. In the same month, March 1979, Urael Lorenzen, secretary at NATO headquarters in Brussels to the man who planned all NATO military exercises, fled with her lover to East Berlin, and appeared on TV to accuse the West of having contingency plans which would reduce much of Central Europe – on both sides of the Iron Curtain – to a nuclear wasteland. Ursel, 38, took with her dossiers from NATO files, and security chiefs in Belgium described her betrayal as 'a devastating blow'.

Western spycatchers stepped up surveillance of possible ravens. They flooded the press with stories of how Communist agents signed on innocently at language schools and seduced girls studying to increase their qualifications for service in multi-national organisations. They put up posters in all NATO and government offices warning: 'There is a code word which opens safes – it is LOVE.' And for a while, the precautions seemed to work. Then, in April 1980, Belgian secretary Imelda Verrept failed to return to her job at NATO headquarters in Brussels after the Easter break. Imelda was in her thirties. She had an attentive new boyfriend. And she had gone away for the holiday with him to East Berlin. Shapex, a major military exercise to be held within weeks by NATO armies, was no longer a mystery to Moscow. Yet another raven had flown after cultivating a cuckoo in the West's nest.

But Russia's most sensational success in exploiting sex for espionage ends was not due to the work of randy ravens, sensuous swallows or manipulating madames. The Kremlin simply cashed in ruthlessly when a man who should have known better took a fancy to a girl he met purely by chance.

Martin Maput Mystery

Along with Sambha espionage scandal, another spying incident came to light. This scandal did not create ripples as the attention of all the countries was riveted on the Sambha scandal. Naturally, this scandal receded into background and many mysteries remained unsolved. The first one was the link between Iran-born Martin and the Soviet Union. Martin was able to secure business worth billions of rupees for his employers. Another facet of this intriguing episode was that Maput, who was born in Russia, could get service in the Indian army. Nobody knows what he did there till his retirement

Martin

The morning of January 16, 1979, was unusually cool and foggy in Calcutta. There was hardly any sign of activity or Traffic at that time of early morning on Park Street. A jeep stopped before an old and magnificent building known as Park Mansions. Five persons got down from the jeep and stood before flat No.20 in that building. They rang the door bell. A short time after, a fair, middle aged, flabby and bespectacled man stood before them and asked, "What do you want?"

"We wish to see Shri Karo Upkar Martin. Is he in?" one of the five men told.

"I am Martin," the man identified himself. The visitors handed him a paper.

"It is alright, you may search the house. In the meantime, I will have my breakfast," replied Martin as his face turned dark. Even then, he tried his best not to lose his composure as he turned into the house with his visitors.

The five started searching the place. This was during the period when India was under Janta government. It is alleged that at that time CIA had launched an operation to uncover Russian agents in India. Probably the Central Intelligence Department was tipped by some such contact that the retired army officer Maput was a Soviet citizen. He was a former Russian agent and after his retirement from the army was again working as their agent. Maput was living in the posh colony of Ramkrishnapuram in South Delhi.

The Research and Analysis wing (RAW) which kept a strict watch on foreign agents, suspected Maput for some time. But they could not collect any worthwhile evidence against him. Anyway, Maput was kept under surveillance for months. The suspicions of RAW were confirmed after keeping an eye on Maput's activities for some time. It was now certain that Maput was indulging in anti-national activities. He was eventually arrested on January 15, 1979, under section 126-B of the Indian Penal Code and sections 3, 5 and 9 of Official Secrets Act.

Martin with Chief Minister Jyoti Basu.

During the interrogation of Maput, it was revealed that he had close relations with Karo Martin and that they worked in conjunction. Martin was working in Mcleod & Co., a very well known firm of Calcutta.

The search at Martin's place was a direct sequel of information gathered from Maput's interrogation. The search party consisted of Intelligence officers, Vibhuti Nandi and Raghubir Singh. Two Calcutta based Intelligence officers, Alok

Ghosh and Prasum Sanyal were assisting them. Vishwajit Chakravarty, the Station House officer of Park Street Police Station also accompanied the Intelligence officers. The search lasted for well over six hours from 10 a.m. to 4 p.m.

The following documents and articles were seized during the search. They were files of confidential correspondence, diaries containing names and addresses of important people, one Russian movie camera, membership card No. 1706 of Army club in Fort William, military map of Cairo, Visa card No. 1174-68421 of Canada, international driving license No. R-130. Apart from them, cheque book No. 253-530 of Sweden Credit Bank, documents pertaining to correspondence of the former Defence Production Minister M.M. Thomas and correspondence file of Calcutta-based, Soviet Commercial Advisor, E. Ejov with Martin, were also seized.

After the arrest, Martin was removed to the office of Special Intelligence situated at No. 15, Lord Sinha Road. He was kept there for the night. It transpired that he had relations with important people abroad. He was making frequent trips to foreign countries. He was particularly visiting Russia and other eastern European countries of the Communist bloc.

Karo Upkar Martin had come to India in 1941. He did his matriculation from here and got the job in 1941 in Calcutta firm, Messrs. M.M. Ispahani & Co. in 1960, he joined another firm, Messrs. Amba Lal, after passing the examination of F.C.I., from Bombay's British Institutes. This company benefitted a lot from his association. During 1965-70, he worked in Sahu Jain & Co. According to police records, he got orders worth billions for this company from Soviet Union. Karo Martin rejoined Mcleod & Co., in 1975, and had been working there since then. It was alleged that he was instrumental in getting orders worth billions of rupees for this company from Communist countries.

Martin was a bachelor and lived with his mother and sister named Zyron. But, his life was neither lonely nor dull. He was member of almost all the elite clubs in Calcutta. He spent his nights with lovely women and spent money lavishly. He never returned to his house before midnight. A beautiful lady named Sonali accompanied him to the Fort William Club. Every month, he used to spend a few nights in a posh hotel on Park Street or Jawaharlal Nehru Road. During these nights, he always had the company of foreign men and women.

Though his salary was Rs.4,000 per month, he donated more than this amount in charities. He spent extravagantly in hotels, gambling dens, and in travels. He maintained cordial relations with the rich and also with political leaders in Bengal.

Everything that Martin confessed to or divulged was kept a secret. Only this much could be found out that he collected information regarding military matters and trade at Delhi and Calcutta. He had supplied details about coal mines and location of other minerals to foreign countries.

Morarji Desai, the then Prime Minister, ordered for deportation of Leonid Andreiwitch, the Soviet Trade Commissioner, and Yuri Rajiwin, third secretary of the Soviet Embassy, when the matter was brought to his notice. Martin was taken to Delhi.

But, nobody knows about the fate of Maput, who got recruited to the Indian army inspite of being a Russian. What happened to him still remains a mystery.

The Spy Scandal that Ruined Profumo

Intrigued by shrieks of laughter from his stately home's swimming pool, Lord Astor guided his weekend guests towards the gate in the pool fence. They pushed it open just as a dazzling beauty emerged, naked from the water. She brushed her long, flowing dark red hair from her eyes — and then noticed the arrival of strangers. Their smiles broadened as she screamed for her swimming costume, and her companions threw it further from her. But the events of the next two years were to wipe those smiles from the faces of almost everyone present. The innocent fun of that summer afternoon in 1961 was to result in the disgrace of a British Government minister, the electoral defeat of his party after 13 years in power, the death of one of those present, serious doubts about a top spymaster, and praise and promotion for a Soviet agent. For the poolside frolic was the opening scene in the British political scandal of the century — the Profumo affair. And it is now clear that what Prime Minister Harold Macmillan at first described as 'a silly scrape over a woman' was, in fact, a carefully orchestrated Russian subversion triumph.

The beauty in the pool was Christine Keeler, then 20. She was staying at a cottage on Lord Astor's Cliveden estate with Dr Stephen Ward, an osteopath whose 'healing hands' had eased the pains of some of the richest and most powerful figures in British society. Lord Astor, grateful for past services, had given him use of the cottage in 1950. Now that generous gesture was to rebound on him savagely. For among his own party of weekend guests was War Minister John Profumo. And he was captivated by the lithe body so temptingly on display before him. Within days he had asked Ward to arrange a rendezvous with Christine. Soon she and the politician were lovers.

Such secret liaisons are not unusual among married members of Parliament. Labour security spokesman George Wigg, who played a leading role in the subsequent scandal, said: 'Few in the House of Commons have not been guilty of some sexual turpitude.' What caused Profumo's downfall was the identity of Ward's other companion that weekend at Cliveden. He was Captain Eugene Ivanov, a GRU master spy masquerading as assistant naval attache at the Russian embassy in London.

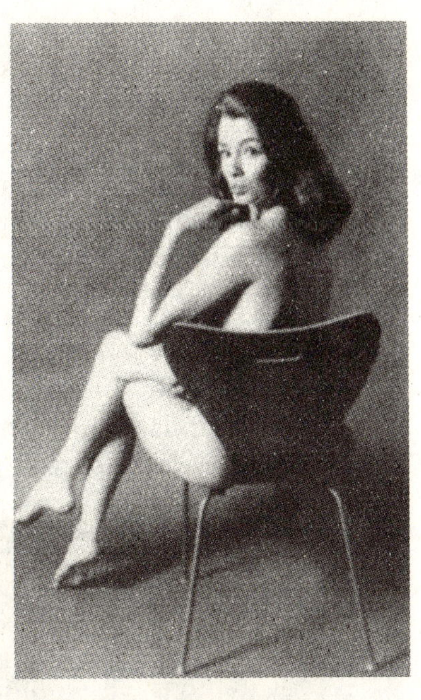

Ward had been introduced to him by Sir Colin Coote, the editor of Lord Astor's newspaper, *The Daily Telegraph.* The osteopath treated him for lumbago, and happened to mention that, as a keen artist, he was anxious to go sketching in Moscow, but was having problems obtaining a visa. When Ivanov toured the *Telegraph's* Fleet Street offices with a party of military attaches, Sir Colin remembered the conversation, and arranged a dinner for the two to meet. They quickly became friends. But unknown to the editor, neither man was what he seemed. And that was to prove catastrophic for Profumo.

One of Ward's sidelines was meeting young girls on the London nightclub circuit, and grooming them into high class prostitutes. Christine Keeler was a nude dancer at the Murray Cabaret Club when she fell under his hypnotic spell. Ward provided girls for visiting international dignitaries as well as his influential patients, and MI5 checked him out since he was moving in powerful circles. They were prepared to turn a blind eye to some of his less savoury antics in return for occasional information. And when he told of his acquaintances with Ivanov, MI5 chief Sir Roger Hollis hatched a bizarre plot to persuade the Soviet to defect. Ivanov was a known spy – double agent Oleg Penkovsky named him during debriefings by British and American interrogators – and Ward was ordered to ply him with Western luxuries, cultivating his passion for drink and women. Christine Keeler was one of those who shared his bed.

Sadly for MI5, Ivanov was a committed Communist who soon saw through the attempted entrapment. Ward, who had some socialist sympathies, may even have told him of it. The Russian reported the situation to Moscow while

playing along with Hollis's scheme. He discovered that, in addition to providing girls for important people, Ward also took pictures of them making love through two-way mirrors. Ivanov obtained copies from three albums of incriminating photographs collected by the osteopath, and his masters for possible blackmail attempts. And when he found that Keeler was Profumo's mistress, he hinted that, if she coaxed from the minister the date on which America planned to equip West Germany's air force with nuclear weapons, Ward would have no more trouble getting his visa for Moscow.

There is no evidence that Keeler ever asked the question, and no suggestion that Profumo would have answered if she had. But news of what was in Ivanov's mind forced Sir Roger Hollis to act. Puzzlingly, he did not go to the War Minister himself, or the Prime Minister, or the Home Secretary, to whom he was directly responsible. Instead he told Cabinet Secretary Sir Norman Brook of Profumo's invidious position – then, astonishingly, asked Sir Norman if he would try to persuade Profumo to help in inducing Ivanov to defect. It was a ploy fraught with danger. No minister could be seen dabbling in espionage, let alone caught trying to subvert a foreign national, and Profumo had the good sense to reject the idea out of hand. At the same time, he decided to end his affair with Keeler, but unwisely did so by letter, using the word Darling. It was to be another nail in his political coffin and in any case, it was too late for Profumo to wriggle out of his predicament.

The Opposition Labour Party was already sniping at the Tory Government over a series of spy scandals – the Portland ring, Admiralty spy William Vassall and double agent George Blake. George Wigg was spearheading the attack. On 11 November 1962, he received a mysterious phone call at the home of his political agent in Dudley. A muffled voice said: 'Forget Vassall, you want to look at Profumo.' Wigg and Profumo were not on the best of terms. They had clashed angrily in the Commons days earlier over the lack of heat acclimatisation given to British troops before duty in the Middle East. But the call had not come from a political aide. In fact, Wigg, who died in August 1983, never found out who made it. It could have been a journalist anxious to bring unprintable rumour into the public spotlight. Equally, it could have been a mischief maker with a grudge against the War Minister. But security experts believe the call came from a Russian agent, intent on causing a scandal. If that was the Kremlin's aim, they were not kept waiting long.

Wigg and his aides began checking on Profumo. Christine Keeler confirmed she had been mistress of both the minister and Ivanov. And it was on the security danger rather than the moral issue of adultery that Wigg launched his assault with a Commons question on 21 March 1963. Labour Party chiefs and the whole of Fleet Street knew a scandal was inevitable. But Home Secretary Henry Brooke, to whom the Wigg question was addressed, was completely in the dark. Profumo foolishly denied any affair with Keeler. Then Brooke summoned Sir Roger Hollis, and demanded to know what was going on. The MI5 chief at last revealed what he had learned 18 months earlier – that Ivanov had asked Ward to get him the date of nuclear arms being given to Germany – but maintained that any security fears ended when Ivanov fled back to Moscow in January 1963, tipped off about the impending storm.

The Government, ill-informed by its top spymaster, now had its back to the wall. Christine Keeler had become involved with two West Indian lovers, one of whom was arrested for beating up the other and jealously firing shots at the home of Stephen Ward. Keeler, hard up for money, approached Fleet Street papers, offering to sell her story. She handed over Profumo's letter. Then she too fled the growing pressure. There were ugly rumours that the Establishment had got rid of her. She was traced to Madrid, still ready to tell her side of events for cash. Profumo continued to deny the affair. He lied to the House of Commons in a statement, and successfully sued an Italian magazine for libel when it doubted his word. But this was not a political squall that would blow over. Profumo went off to Venice on holiday with his wife, former actress Valerie Hobson. He decided to clear his conscience with her. They returned immediately to London where, on June 4, he resigned as War Minister and as an MP – a job he had held for 25 years. His disgrace for contempt of the Commons was complete when his name was removed from the Privy Council.

The scandal was now at full flood, fuelled by the revelations of Christine Keeler, who sold her memoirs to a sensational Sunday newspaper for £23,000, and the sensational death of Stephen Ward. He took a drugs overdose in July while on bail facing charges of living on immoral earnings. He was described at his trial as a 'thoroughly filthy fellow' and 'a wicked, wicked creature'. But Sir Colin Coote, the man who made the ill-fated introduction to Ivanov, said: 'I should doubt whether a more trivial person has ever seriously embarrassed a government.' In fact, it became increasingly clear that both Ward and Keeler had merely been pawns in the game.

The House of Commons held a full debate on the Profumo affair on 17 June. Prime Minister Harold Macmillan was mercilessly mauled. He was forced to admit that no one had told him what was happening until it was too late to change the course of events. It was a staggering confession from the head of a government, and even arch antagonist George Wigg was embarrassed as he watched his political foe reeling from the twin blows of betrayed loyalty to a colleague and an appalling lack of information. Macmillan resigned as Conservative leader within 12 months, and many believe the Profumo debacle was a significant factor in the 1964 General Election defeat of his successor, Sir Alec Douglas Home, by Harold Wilson and the Labour Party.

M15 chief Sir Roger Hollis watched Macmillan stumble through his Commons ordeal from the public gallery. He too was to retire within a year, possibly under pressure from members of Macmillan's Cabinet who felt he was grossly at fault for keeping them in the dark about Profumo's predicament and the fact that Ivanov had proved to be a spy worthy of expulsion. Later it was learned that Sir Roger had specifically forbidden full investigation of Ivanov's activities by MI5.

Sir Roger died in October 1973. Eight years later, writer Chapman Pincher analysed his career in the book "Their Trade Is Treachery". He said that the spymaster had done as little as possible and as late as possible in the Profumo affair. He also accused him of doctoring a report of his interview with 1945 defector Igor Gouzenko; inexplicably suspending interrogation of Anthony Blunt for two weeks in 1964, thus giving the traitor time to consult his masters or destroy evidence; refusing to pursue inquiries against some of the men named as spies by Blunt; and presiding over MI5 at a time of conspicuous lack of success, partly because all anti-Communist operations were leaked to the targets. Pincher then pointed out that for more than a decade, Soviet defectors were terrified of coming to Britain because they knew of a Russian mole in a powerful position. And he made the devastating claim that Sir Roger, a trusted agent for 25 years, was that mole.

Prime minister Margaret Thatcher denied the allegation in the House of Commons in 1981. And Sir Roger was also cleared of blame in Lord Denning's Committee of Inquiry report into the Profumo affair, issued in 1964. Perhaps he had given plausible explanations for the actions which so angered the Cabinet. Perhaps his role was minimised to avoid publicising MI5, which is still officially non-existent. But there was an implied reproach for an unwise attempt to induce a defection in these words from Lord Denning:

'Captain Ivanov filled a new role in Russian technique. It was to divide the United Kingdom from the United States by devious means. If ministers or prominent people can be placed in compromising positions, or made the subject of damaging rumour, or the security service can be made to appear incompetent, it may weaken the confidence of the United States in our integrity and reliability. If this was the object of Captain Ivanov, with Ward as his tool, he succeeded only too well.'

The meaning was clear. Hollis had continued to play with fire when he should have known better.

The Russians had not created the Profumo scandal, but they had manipulated it to full advantage. More evidence of their wiles emerged in America. A KGB officer working at the United Nations was providing the FBI with information which spymaster J. Edgar Hoover valued highly. In 1963, he told the FBI of a talk in Moscow with Ivanov, who claimed he had bugged Christine Keeler's bedroom, and gained valuable intelligence from her pillow talk with Profumo. Hoover sent the information to President Kennedy, but he declined to forward it to London, telling aides: 'Mr Macmillan is in enough trouble already.' In the event, the UN double agent was proved to be a stooge, feeding mischievous misinformation.

The fact that his career had been destroyed by a cynical Soviet scheme was no consolation for John Profumo, who withdrew from the spotlight with as much dignity as he could muster, and devoted his life to unpublicised charity work. He was ruined by his sexual appetite just as surely as those politicians and diplomats trapped by swallows and ravens. But at least he survived after getting caught up in the shadowy world of espionage.

The Fatal Umbrella

Fear shot through the heart of Georgi Sergeevich Okolovich when he opened the door of his Frankfurt home on 18 February 1954, and he was confronted by a burly Russian. Okolovich, a leader of the prominent anti-Communist Soviet emigre group NTS, had survived two earlier kidnap attempts. Now it seemed Moscow had decided on more drastic action. The visitor, who introduced himself as Nikolai Chochlov, had written orders from the Communist Party Central Committee for Okolovich's execution. But after showing his victim the death warrant, Chochlov asked him to ring the West German authorities. And what he later told them was soon front page news around the world.

Chochlov, a secret service veteran, had sent dozens of men into free Europe to kill or kidnap influential critics of the Kremlin or refugees from the Russian regime. But when he himself was ordered to carry out a 'wet affair' – spy jargon for liquidating an enemy of the state – he knew it was his chance to escape. American and German counter-intelligence men arrested his two accomplices. Then Chochlov led them into woods outside Munich. There, hidden inside a car battery, was what seemed like a gold cigarette case. Chochlov demonstrated its real use – as an electric pistol which noiselessly fired dum-dum bullets coated in potassium cyanide.

At first the KGB merely tried to discredit their former agent. Moscow announced that his story was a CIA invention, that he and Okolovich were relatives and both Nazi war criminals. When Chochlov continued to speak out, more lethal steps were taken. In September 1957, he collapsed at a Frankfurt meeting with violent stomach pains and nausea. Within days of entering hospital, he was covered in hideous dark brown stripes and blotches, and black and blue swellings. Blood seeped through pores of his dry, shrunken skin. His hair fell out by the handful.

Suspecting poisoning by the toxic metal thallium, German doctors tried every known antidote without success. As the victim's bones decayed and his blood turned to plasma, Okolovich was told there was no hope for the man who had spared his life. But the reprieved Russian exile refused to give up. He persuaded a local American hospital to take over the case. Six top military surgeons began round-the-clock treatment at a heavily-guarded U.S. Army camp. For a week massive injections of cortisone, vitamins, steroids and experimental drugs, plus continuous blood transfusions, kept the patient alive. Then, slowly, almost miraculously, he began to recover. By late October, totally bald and badly scarred, he was off the danger list.

Toxicologists later discovered exactly why Chochlov's complaint had been so difficult to cure. He had been poisoned with thallium exposed to intense atomic radiation, which made the metal disintegrate almost instantly through the system, destroying the white corpuscles of the blood and draining the body's life-sustaining fluids. Chochlov had been more than lucky to survive. Later victims of Eastern bloc poison attacks were not so fortunate.

On the evening of 7 September 1978, Georgi Markov was waiting for a bus on London's Waterloo Bridge after finishing work at the BBC World Service building nearby. Suddenly he felt a sharp pain in his thigh. Turning, he saw a man picking up an umbrella he had apparently dropped. The man mumbled an apology before leaping into a taxi. Markov went home for a quiet dinner with his wife. At bedtime, he began to feel unwell, and mentioned the umbrella incident to her for the first time. By 2 p.m., his temperature had reached 104° F and an ambulance rushed him to hospital. He died there four days later.

At first the mysterious fever and nausea baffled doctors. Then an inch-by-inch search of the body using a magnifying glass revealed a tiny metal ball, measuring just 1.52 millimetres in diameter. The ball, made of a platinum and iridium mixture used in jet engines, had been expertly drilled with two microscopic connecting holes 0.35 mm wide. And they had been filled with ricin, a by-product of the process of extracting oil from the castor oil plant, and twice as deadly as cobra venom. There was then no known antidote.

Detectives found it impossible to trace the taxi driver, or witnesses from the bus queue. But painstakingly they built up a picture of what had happened. And the Battersea inquest was sufficiently convinced to record a verdict of unlawful killing.

Georgi Markov was a Bulgarian-born author and playwright who fled his homeland in June 1969, after a satirical stage performance he wrote upset the authorities. He became a broadcaster in the West, never afraid to speak his mind in radio transmissions to the Eastern bloc from both Britain and West Germany. 'He hated the regime,' his widow told the inquest. Increasingly, the regime of Bulgaria, the most Stalinist Soviet satellite country, hated his attacks. And in August 1978, a hit-man travelled to Western Europe with a double mission. In Paris he fired a pellet into the back of Bulgarian radio and TV reporter Vladimir Kostov during a Metro journey. Kostov was lucky – not enough of the poison, manufactured mainly in Czechoslovakia and Hungary – had been used and he survived after an agonising battle in hospital.

Two weeks later there were no mistakes on Waterloo Bridge. Nobody noticed the pellet hit Markov, fired, it is believed, by a surgical implantation gun concealed in the umbrella tip. And had the victim not gasped, 'I have been poisoned, murdered,' as the lethal ricin more than doubled his white blood-cell count, the West might never have learned of yet another sinister Soviet bloc murder method.

Scotland Yard officers believed the assassination was organised independently by Bulgarian espionage agents, and Whitehall sources claimed the Russians were furious at the bad publicity it caused. But Western spycatchers remembered the Politburo orders following the Stashinsky defection, and began re-evaluating other sudden 'natural deaths'. One in particular has always concerned security chiefs.

On 18 January 1963, Hugh Gaitskell, moderate leader of the British Labour Party, died in hospital of systemic lupus erythematosus, a failure of the heart and kidneys. It was a complaint hardly ever seen in men over 40 in temperate climates, yet Gaitskell, 56, had contracted it less than a month after being released from hospital after treatment for viral pneumonia. Then Soviet defector Anatoli Golitsin told interrogators that, before he fled, the chief of the KGB's northern Europe section mentioned plans to kill an opposition party leader. And MI5 investigators discovered that, shortly before his death, Gaitskell had visited the Russian embassy in London to collect a visa for a trip to Moscow, and had been given coffee and biscuits.

Experts at Britain's Microbiological Research Establishment at Porton Down, Wiltshire, could not say how the disease might be caused — but CIA spymaster James Angleton discovered Soviet medical papers announcing success in experiments with a drug that could induce fatal heart and kidney failure. Though Gaitskell's widow and most of his Labour Party colleagues continued to believe the death was natural, top espionage men, including MI5 chief Sir Martin Furnival Jones, kept an open mind. Gaitskell had fought hard to stop the Party swinging to the Left. Under his successors, extremist Marxists openly flaunted their views under Labour's banner.

Sambha Espionage Scandal

This is one of the most sensational and complicated spy scandal in free India. It is supposed to be a case of selling secret informations by arm of officers. If that was so, why were so many manoeuvres made? The whole thing got enmeshed in moves and counter-moves. Then, inspite of best efforts made, no convincing evidence could be produced. Why? Were all the officers charged in this case guilty? Was this matter as simple as it seemed to be? Verily, it was a very complicated spy scandal that had many loose ends about which nothing will ever be revealed.

It was a sudden move. Major Uppal covered the face of Captain Rathore with a hood similar to that which hangmen usually use to cover the face of the person to be executed. The entire face of the convict is covered by it and it reaches up to his neck. Captain Rathore was totally non-plussed. "What is this?" he asked in a voice choked with emotion.

The Major replied in a cold and stem voice, "Your game is up Captain. You stand exposed for spying."

This happened on August 24, 1978. The place was India's capital, Delhi. Captain Ranbir Singh Rathore was returning after meeting Col. Grewal of the Military Intelligence Directorate. The Captain was posted at Kamptee in Maharashtra and had been called to Delhi. As he reached Army Headquarters, he was met by Major Uppal at the main entrance. The Major told him that his son had been admitted to the Army Hospital. Could Captain Rathore reach him there in his jeep? The Major had an escort of a few armed soldiers. The Captain turned the jeep towards Delhi cantonment. At a lonely spot in South Delhi, the jeep was stopped and Captain Rathore was asked to sit at the back.

Around 10.30 in the night, Captain Rathore was locked up in the Military Intelligence Interrogation Cell in civilian clothes. His interrogation started as soon as he felt sleepy. He was not allowed to sleep and searching questions about the spy ring were put to him. A few months after his interrogation, raids were conducted at Delhi, Junglot, Jammu, Nagarkota and many other places on the India-Pakistan border on the night between 22-23 January, 1979. A total of fifty three army officers were arrested during these raids.

There had been no reaction in Pakistan, when Captain Rathore was arrested on 24th August, 1978. But, as the news of the arrest of army officers in India reached them, there was an unusual reaction there. 107 army officers were arrested by Pakistan Military Intelligence in Lahore, Sialkot, Karachi and Rawalpindi. They were all charged with the offence of spying for India. The trial of these officers was rushed through. After a summary trial for three days by the military courts, two Colonels, three Majors and a sepoy were hanged. The rest were hanged or sentenced to imprisonment at a later date. It is supposed that the Indian spy network was nearly wiped out after these arrests and trials.

Actually, Sambha is the name of a small town located on the Pathankot Jammu highway. No. 168 Infantry Brigade of the 39th Infantry Division is posted there. That is why it was also called Sambha Brigade. The entire Sambha Brigade became involved in this affair and as such this episode was given the name of Sambha espionage scandal. Apart from men of Military intelligence, agents of other secret services were also stationed in Sambha. The agents of Pakistani army and other secret services of that country are very active in this area. This area has strategic importance for both the countries.

Captain Rathore, who has been mentioned in the beginning of this article was posted for internal spying in the Sambha Brigade on behalf of 527 Intelligence & Field Security Company from the year 1974 to 1976. Together with him, Major S.C. Jolly of 16th Corp of Nagarkota and

Major R.P. Madan of Eastern Command did espionage work in Pakistan with the help of informers.

This can only be called as a strange quirk of fate that Captain Rathore who had been warmly praised for his good work in 1977, was now charged and arraigned as a double agent working for Pakistan since 1977. His own former associates, Major Jolly, Major Madan, Major Solanki and Major Talwar were entrusted with the enquiry of the case. Captain Rathore later retreated from his statement given earlier. He claimed that he was tortured to confess that Captain Nangiyal and gunner Aya Singh took him to Pakistan on the night of July 30-31, 1974.

Apart from Captain Rathore, Captain A.K. Rana, Who had been an officer in the Military Intelligence Department of Sambha Brigade till 1978, was also charged for being a spy of Pakistan. Captain Rana had been posted in 168 Sambha Brigade on 5th January, 1976 and remained there till March, 1978. He had replaced Captain Rathore. Rana was arrested after Captain Rathore divulged a lot of details regarding this espionage network on October 27, 1978. His confessional statement, that formed the basis for the arrest of Captain Rana ran as follows, "I went to Pakistan on January 11, 1976 and also on July 19, 1976. I took Captain Rana with me. There, I introduced him to Major Akbar Khan of Pakistan's Military Intelligence Branch."

Nobody knows the activities of the Military Intelligence Branch till the arrest of 53 army officers on the night of January 22-23, 1979. But this is certain that the most of the arrested officers were connected with Sambha Brigade during 1974-78 or with Captain Rathore and Captain Rana in some way or the other. Another 90 army men belonging to 527 Intelligence and Field Security were also taken into custody.

From information gathered from knowledgeable sources, it was surmised that Captain Rathore was called to Delhi and arrested under a well thought out plan. Prior to this,

Captain Nangiyal had also been arrested in 1975. He was suspected to be a Pakistani spy, but no evidence was found against him. The persons who testified against him in 1976, happened to be Naik Sarban Das and gunner Aya Singh. Aya Singh had told the higher officers that Captain Nangiyal had taken Captain Rathore to Pakistan. He had become approver in that case. In this way, gunner Aya Singh was playing two roles—that of an accused and as well as an approver. The other person who appeared as a witness against Captain Nangiyal was Naik Sarban Das. He had been sentenced to six months' imprisonment twice by the Military Court. This was clear from his record.

Naik Sarban Das was arrested again for some offence, when he was posted in 31st Division at Jhansi. From there he absconded. Later, he was arrested by a police inspector Sewa Singh, of Jammu and Kashmir. He was apprehended on the border. He posed to be a Major in Pakistani army and had a revolver with him.

On the previous occasion, the charge that he was a Pakistani spy could not be proved, but this time he was sentenced to seven years' imprisonment for absconding from the prison. Later on, this man became an important witness in the Sambha espionage scandal. Aya Singh had also been sentenced to seven years' imprisonment in March, 1978, on charge of desertion from the army. Aya Singh became an approver in this case and was fully co-operating with the enquiry commission as a key witness. It was during his interrogation that the names of Captain Rathore and Captain Rana cropped up.

Major General H.K. Kaul, who was Director of Military Intelligence was removed from his post and sent elsewhere. The commander of 39th Division of Sambha Brigade, Major General K. Gauri Shankar, was posted in his place.

Havaldar P.P. Singh who was personal assistant of commander D.P. Nayer of the Sambha Brigade was sentenced to 14 years' imprisonment. Major Jolly and Major

Madan, who had worked with Captain Rathore in 1977 and appreciated his work, were absolved of all charges. As a matter of fact, they had investigated into this scandal. It is really strange that only these two officers were found to be capable and trustworthy in the whole army to enquire into this scandal. Captain Talwar, who had worked as a junior to Captain Rathore was also associated with the enquiry. He had taken out Sarban Das and Aya Singh from the prison and kept them in his custody. It was Captain Talwar who helped them in their evidence. Was there some mystery involved in these affairs?

But the biggest surprise in this scandal was that inspite of so much uproar in the country over this scandal, the Defence Minister, Jagjiwan Ram, did not order an enquiry by the Intelligence Department. The Home Minister, Y.B. Chavan had suggested this to the defence minister and army authorities. For reasons best known to them they did not do it. Was it to shield some higher ups? The result was that truth could never be unravelled and this scandal remains an unsolved mystery.

Sushma – Suresh Episode

There are many questions that remain unresolved in this Sambha espionage scandal. Why did the then defence Minister, Jagitwan Ram, shy away from an enquiry into the sordid affair by the Central Bureau as suggested by Y.B. Chavan, who was the Home Minsiter at that time. How could Pakistan launch an operation to wipe out the Indian counterespionage cell on the night of January 22-23, 1979? Who informed them of the Indian action the same day? Why did the Pakistan authorities suspect their officers and men, numbering 107, immediately after the arrest of Captain Rathore on August 24, 1978? Why did the Pakistani authorities try some of their officers hurriedly and sentenced them immediately? Experts believe that some one who had full access to the confidential files and documents sent to the residence of the defence minister was behind all these intriguing incidents. He must have been involved in sending information to foreign intelligence agencies.

Readers must be aware of the Sushma-Suresh episode which became the talk of the town. 'Surya' magazine, edited by Mrs. Maneka Gandhi, published compromising photographs of Suresh, son of defence minsiter Jagjiwan Ram, involving Sushma. The Intelligence officers believed that Suresh must have been blackmailed.

It is also alleged that Suresh came to know many secret affairs and documents due to his influence in the defence ministry, before these incriminating photographs came to light.

But, who is there to tell the truth? The whole thing will remain shrouded in mystery.

The Daring Courage of Elie Cohen

The Jews learned the art of spying the hard way. Centuries of persecution, purges and pogroms developed in them a natural talent for survival in a hostile environment and the cunning ability to keep their real thoughts, feelings and intentions secret while finding out about those of their oppressors. Since Biblical times, Jews have been invaluable agents for every nation with espionage aspirations. Forty years ago, it was the underground activities of the Irgun and Haganah organisations which finally brought to reality the long-held dream of the Jewish homeland in Palestine. And since 1948, the secret services of tiny Israel have become the envy of the world.

Their efficiency has been honed out of necessity – no new state has ever had to fight so many wars against neighbours committed to crushing it – and a passionate patriotism unique among intelligence organisations. The exploits of Israeli agents have won admiration even from their enemies. And no one earned it more than the amazing Elie Cohen.

Cohen was the Egyptian-born son of Syrian parents. He worked as a bookkeeper in Alexandria until 1956, when fear of an anti-Jewish backlash from President Nasser after the disastrous Anglo-French Suez invasion, and fighting between Israel and Egypt, made him decide to move to Tel Aviv. His quick brain and superb memory quickly brought him to the attention of Mossad, the overseas arm of the Israeli secret services.

His training was thorough and ruthlessly professional. Israeli agents are pushed to the limits of physical endurance to test their ability to withstand torture. And Cohen's cover also had to be perfect. For he was to be installed in Damascus, capital of Israel's most consistently hostile neighbour, Syria. He was given a new identity, Kamel Amine Tabet, a Syrian Moslem. And to make his new character convincing, he had to learn a new life story involving birth in the Lebanese capital, Beirut, and emigration to Argentina. Cohen perfected his Syrian accent talking to businessmen in Jerusalem, then flew to Buenos Aires via Zurich.

With discreet Mossad back-up, providing an apartment and ample funds, Cohen quickly established himself in the Syrian community as an ardent, Israeli-hating patriot. He made friends with influential people inside and outside the Syrian embassy in Buenos Aires, and impressed them with generous donations to Arab charities. By early 1962, Mossad felt he was ready for the next step, and ordered him to Damascus. He flew to Italy, took a boat to Beirut, and bribed his way through a Syrian border customs post – he did not want prying officials to find his miniature radio transmitter, codes and invisible inks.

Cohen had no time to follow the classic KGB ploy of lying low and not attracting attention. Tel Aviv wanted results fast, and that meant risking exposure by establishing contacts ostentatiously. Cohen moved into a luxurious villa and began trading as an import-export dealer. He told everyone that he was a Ba'ath Party convert who had come home to help his country, and he backed his words with cash drawn on an American bank. He impressed local big-wigs by importing expensive French mink coats as gifts for their wives. At first, the only danger came from marriage brokers, intent on finding him a suitable bride. Cohen politely declined all offers. Not only did he already have a wife in Israel, but he needed his bachelor privacy in Syria to radio secrets to Tel Aviv.

And there was much to tell. His fierce patriotism earned him the chance to give talks on Radio Damascus, aimed at Syrians overseas in Spanish-speaking countries. He accepted at once. He could now learn from the inside about the Ministry of Information, which provided basic material for the broadcasts, and slip pre-arranged code words into the chats for Israeli ears only. These supplemented his clandestine radio transmissions and the secret messages he smuggled out in 'exports' to Mossad in Argentina.

Cohen made a point of urging stronger defences against Israel whenever he met important people from the ruling military junta. Anxious to prove that his fears were groundless, they gave him conducted tours of the defences on the Golan Heights, and revealed a network of underground tunnels along the Israeli border. Soon senior army officers made Cohen's villa a regular meeting place, particularly after he began to provide girls for them, and tongues wagged freely in the relaxed atmosphere.

Cohen ingratiated himself so well that he became an honourary major in the army, and was given a responsible position in the Ba'ath party. This enabled him to accompany the Prime Minister on visits to other Arab capitals, including Cairo, where he sat in on talks between leaders and their military experts. Soon the successful spy had so much material that he had to get back to Israel to unburden his memory. Using a business trip to Argentina as his cover, he flew to Buenos Aires, stayed a few days, then flew to Europe, and slipped unnoticed back to Tel Aviv. Israel now knew exactly the strength of the Syrian forces facing her, and the intentions of their leaders, as well as the plans and attitudes of Syria's allies.

A Ba'ath party coup soon after Cohen's return to Damascus early in 1963 put the informer in an even stronger position. Several of his closest friends were now ministers, and he was able to keep the Israelis in touch with all the latest government thinking, together with news of arms purchases and army dispositions.

But such staggering success in so short a time sowed the seeds of its own destruction. Perhaps over-confident, Cohen allowed himself to be photographed in the official group when he accompanied the United Arab Republic's commander-in-chief of an inspection of border military posts. Then the Voice of Israel radio station broadcast some secret facts Cohen had provided. It was a stupid mistake, alerting the Syrians to a spy in their midst. And when, months later, Egyptian secret police told their Syrian counterparts that an old schoolfriend had identified Kamel Amine Tabet as an Egyptian Jew from the photograph published in newspapers, the game was over.

Though aware of the spy hunt, Cohen courageously continued to file reports to Tel Aviv. One of his last transmissions told of sabotage teams being trained for infiltration. And he was using the radio on the morning counterespionage men burst into his villa and arrested him.

The repercussions of the arrest were enormous. Cohen was tried in secret, not so much for security reasons as to save embarrassment among Syria's rulers and their furious Arab allies. Two French advocates briefed by Israel were not allowed to defend him, or appeal against the inevitable death sentence. Their protests at this 'defiance of all moral rules' was ignored, as was Israel's unprecedented, top secret offer of army lorries, tractors, medical supplies, ten Syrian spies and more than a million dollars in exchange for one life. Elie

Cohen was publicly hanged under floodlights in Damascus's Martyrs Square at Midnight on 18 May, 1965. His body, mutilated by torture, was buried in the city, and all Israeli requests for its return were rejected.

The master spy's exploits led to the collapse of the government. Cabinet ministers who had befriended him were hounded out of office. Sixty army officers were arrested, and seventeen executed for compromising the safety of the state. But the real damage to Syria only became apparent in 1967 during the Six Day War, when Israeli troops quickly routed the forces that had taunted them so long from the 'impregnable' Golan Heights.

The Champagne Spy

While Elie Cohen was establishing himself in Damascus, an equally ingenious and extraordinary Israeli spy was winning acceptance in the upper echelons of Egyptian high society in Cairo. For four years Wolfgang Lotz, a German-born Jew, conned police, army and espionage chiefs in Gamal Nasser's republic by wining and dining them in a way which earned him the nickname 'The Champagne Spy'. And after sending back a stream of priceless information which helped Israel win the Six Day War, he survived to join the victory celebrations in Tel Aviv.

During the 1950s, Israel was increasingly concerned at the growing number of ex-Nazis hired by Egypt to work on fighter aircraft and rocket missiles. It was clear Nasser intended some devastating strike against his Jewish neighbours. Painstaking detective work by Israeli secret agents all over the world and sympathetic intelligence men in America, France and Germany helped pinpoint the 400 scientists, technicians and engineers involved, and how they were hired. But Israel needed somebody inside Egypt to find out how the work was progressing. It did not take Mossad chiefs long to locate the ideal candidate.

Wolfgang Lotz was the son of a Mannheim theatre impresario and an actress, so playing roles was in his blood.

After his father died, his mother emigrated to Palestine in 1933. At 16, Lotz first tasted undercover work with the Haganah, fighting to protect Jewish villagers, and during World War II he served in the British Army as a Commando, seeing action in the desert battles against Rommel, and picking up Egyptian dialects while stationed in the Suez area. Then he joined the new Israeli army, winning promotion to major after distinguished campaigns in the 1948 war of independence and the 1956 Sinai battles. By I960, he had proved himself ice-cool under pressure. He was fluent in English, Arabic and German. He was also blonde and German-looking. He was just what the Israeli spy masters needed.

Lotz agreed to play the part of a pro-Nasser ex-Nazi who hated Jews. After intensive training in the tricks of the espionage trade – coded messages, invisible ink etc., he was sent back to Germany to perfect his cover. He travelled from city to city, familiarising himself with the latest slang, and the names of sporting and TV stars, for use in small talk. Since he was born in Germany, his life story was based on his real name and birth certificate. It was not too difficult to pretend he had fought with Rommel during the war–he had fought the battles, but on the other side and to hide the fact that he had left Germany in 1933, an 11-year stay in Australia was invented.

Armed with letters of introduction from carefully cultivated new friends met on his return to Germany, Lotz sailed to Egypt as a tourist in January, 1961. Posing as a breeder of top class horses, he asked staff at his Nile-side hotel where he could go riding. They directed him to the Cavalry Club, an exclusive haunt of police and army chiefs. On his first visit, he complimented police general Youssef Ghorab on his horsemanship. Ghorab, delighted with the flattery, invited him to dinner the next night. There he was introduced to other influential guests as 'Germany's top horse breeder'. Everyone was enthusiastic when Lotz said he was considering opening a stud farm in Egypt. And within weeks he was on close terms not only with Ghorab, but with Colonel Abdul

Rahman, deputy head of Egyptian military intelligence, General Fouad Osman, chief of security for Egypt's rocket sites, and many of the Germans working on Nasser's secret projects. He returned to Europe to report to his Mossad masters.

By late 1961, Lotz was back in Egypt, with 17 trunks of luggage and a Volkswagen car. A police colonel escorted him down the gangway from his ship at Alexandria to a typical Arab embrace from General Ghorab. His trunks were waved through customs, and a police escort gave him VIP passage off the crowded quayside. The new German immigrant brought expensive presents for his new friends – stereo record players, tape recorders, coffee makers, food mixers. He also imported something he told no one about – a secret radio transmitter hidden in the heel of one of his riding boots. And, to the delight of the Egyptians, he had acquired a wife.

Marrying Waltraudt Neumann, a busty, blonde who looked typically German, was something of a feat for Lotz because he was already married, to an Israeli girl, the mother of his two children. It took delicate persuasion from Mossad to convince her that Lotz's 'wedding ceremony' in Munich was purely a marriage of convenience, necessary to perfect his cover in Egypt. And Waltraudt proved an invaluable ally for Lotz, helping him host the lavish parties at which champagne loosened tongues, and asking questions which, from Lotz, would have been highly impertinent and suspicious. The Egyptians treated her like a queen, and many would do almost anything for her.

The Lotzes established their stud farm in the fashionable Cairo suburb of Zamalek, on an island in the Nile, and lived first in a nearby apartment, then in a luxurious eight-bedroom villa in Gizeh. They slipped easily into the upper class social round, riding in the morning, lazing by the Cavalry Club swimming pool, sipping cocktails at sunset, partying almost every evening. Lotz stabled some horses at a riding school in Abbasia, and established the habit of climbing a tower by the school's race track to watch them being exercised. From the tower, he also had a perfect view of the Egyptian army's biggest tank depot next door, and could see when tanks were mobilised for action, and which direction they were sent. Livestock deals were also a good excuse for Lotz's periodic trips back to Germany, to pass on what he learned to his spymasters. And his high-up contacts helped him learn a lot.

General Ghorab introduced him to the governor of the Suez Canal zone, and all three toured military installations there in the governor's car. General Osman invited him to inspect rocket bases in the Sinai and Negev deserts and even posed for a portrait in front of one of the rockets on its launching pad. He believed Lotz was just a keen amateur photographer. Once, and Waltraudt took a chance and drove their car down

a prohibited road in the desert between Cairo and Ismailia to check out reports of a secret base there, guards who arrested them were so impressed with the names Lotz gave as people who would vouch for him that the couple were entertained to lunch at the base by the commanding officer.

Top Egyptian army men felt free to share ultra-secret plans at Lotz's parties. Colonel Anwar Sadat, later to succeed Nasser as president, was among the guests coaxed by Lotz to chat about Cairo's intentions against Israel, and the prospects of concerted military action by Middle East nations. Germans working on the feared rocket projects were equally forthcoming. Lulled into a false sense of security by Lotz's pretended nostalgia for the Third Reich, they moaned about technical hitches and the problems of working with Arabs. Lotz was able to monitor progress on the weapons, and pinpoint key workers who were targets later of an Israeli terror campaign involving letter bombs, anonymous phone threats and gun-point warnings. Lotz was so close to the German workers, and so trusted by the Egyptians, that he was asked by General Osman to report on some of the immigrants. When Lotz alleged that one brilliant scientist had no sympathy for Nasser and was working only for the money, the German's six-year contract was cancelled and he was expelled.

Then, quite suddenly, the bubbly life of Israel's champagne superspy went flat. He shrugged off a dinner party conversation in which a West German embassy attache said he could not remember Lotz being a member of Rommel's Afrika Korps. But on February 22, 1965, counterespionage agents were waiting for him and Waltraudt when they returned to their villa after spending the weekend with General Ghorab. The Egyptians had discovered the couple's new radio transmitter, a larger and more powerful model concealed in a pair of bathroom scales. And they had a complete dossier of their messages to Tel Aviv over three years. Their praise – 'You were the best spy ever to work in Egypt' – was small consolation to Lotz for being caught.

The Egyptians later claimed that Lotz gave himself away through carelessness. They said security men checking every house along the route to be used for an official visit by East German leader Walter Ulbricht had been let into Lotz's villa by a servant, and found the radio and codes lying about. A more likely explanation for the spy's demise is that Lotz was 'blown' by one of the Russian agents who infiltrated West German intelligence in the 1960s. The Israelis needed German help to establish Lotz's bona fides in Egypt, and later cooperated closely with Bonn in the hope that the government there would persuade Germans not to work for Nasser. And by 1965, Russia was anxious to impress the Egyptian leader.

Once he realised that the game was up, Lotz concentrated on saving his own life and protecting Waltraudt. He knew that if the Egyptians discovered he was an Israeli, he would be executed, just as Elie Cohen was a few months later in Syria. In his favour was the fact that, unusually for a Jew, he was uncircumcised. Both he and Waltraudt were tortured, but both maintained they were West Germans, and Lotz convinced his captors that his 'wife' had little to do with the espionage. Shortly before the trial, he grabbed the chance of a propaganda TV appearance to declare: 'If the Israelis want to spy in Egypt, they should send their own people there.' It confirmed his non-Jewishness in Arab eyes, while telling Tel Aviv that his cover had not been broken.

Though playing the role of the remorseful agent saved him from death, Lotz was still sentenced to 25 years hard labour in the notoriously tough Tura penitentiary near Cairo. Waltraudt was jailed for three years as an accomplice. West German consul officials visited both, helping to maintain the fiction of their nationality. And Bonn was also involved in the delicate negotiations which resulted in Lotz being freed on February 3, 1968. He and nine Israeli servicemen were exchanged for 500 of the 4,400 Egyptian prisoners-of-war held by Israel.

The Cairo authorities insisted as part of the deal that Lotz be returned to West Germany as a German citizen. And he was duly handed his airline tickets to exile by the West German consul. But when the Lufthansa flight to Frankfurt stopped over in Athens, Lotz and Waltraudt left the plane and secretly returned to Tel Aviv, unsung heroes whose information had played a crucial part in Israel's stunning Six Day War victory eight months earlier.

Ramswaroop Scandal

An astonishing tale of a man who was charged on the grounds of international espionage. During his thirty years stint in espionage, he was said that he amassed wealth disproportionate to his known sources of income. Not only that, he had contacts with the then Prime Minister Morarji Desai and many foreign dignitaries. This spy scandal left the entire country shocked as the evil deeds of foreign powers were exposed.

Ram Swaroop

Ramswaroop somehow got to know that the government knew about his nefarious activities. The officers of intelligence agencies were in hot pursuit and the time was not far off when they would tighten the noose round his neck. He also knew that he would be arrested under Official Secrets Act or Foreign Exchange Regulation Act (FERA). To avoid such an eventuality, he started moving the courts for anticipatory bail.

It was on 28th October, 1985, that the police could trace him in a guest house in New Friend's Colony. He was staying there under the assumed name of Prem Kumar Chopra. It was found that he had been hiding himself at different places under different names for some time. The police started investigations into his antecedents.

Pran Nath Lekhi came forward as defence counsel for the accused Satwant Singh in the Indira Gandhi murder case. For security as well as many other reasons, the intelligence department thought it fit to keep the activities of Lekhi under surveillance. During this surveillance, it transpired that Lekhi had close contacts with suspect Ramswaroop. When the matter war further investigated, the spying activities of Ramswaroop were laid bare for all to see.

Ramswaroop, aged 55, had come to Delhi from Lahore after the partition. He stayed in a servant's quarter near the residences of the members of the parliament on North Avenue. For a living he started fixing punctures in cycles. He courted a Chinese woman and persuaded her to marry him. It is another matter that this alliance did not last long.

According to the information gathered by the intelligence agencies, he was working for the American intelligence agency CIA for at least fifteen years. He used to offer the bait of foreign travel to people in exchange for divulging secret information to him.

According to the charge sheet presented in the court, Ramswaroop seemed to have come into big money in the early part of the seventh decade. He had become very popular with American agents because of his capacity for hard work, perseverance and dedication to espionage work. In 1967, his case officer Schneider had so much confidence in him that he entrusted Ramswaroop to work on Morarji Desai and persuade him to resign from Mrs. Gandhi's cabinet. It is said that when the American diplomat Harry C. Weatherbee was asked to leave India in the aftermath of Larkins' spy scandal, he did so after instructing Ramswaroop. Ramswaroop was getting a salary of Rs. 20,000 per month apart from another substantial amount per month for expenses. He had even floated a news agency and under its cover sent cuttings of important news to Helsinki, Frankfurt and America for evaluation and analysis.

Ramswaroop met one agent, code-named King at the American Information Centre some twenty years' back.

He used to go there for collecting necessary material. King offered to pay him Rs. 400 for bringing details of the personal lives of the employees at the centre. Subsequently, King induced him to work for CIA. Ramswaroop supplied his American masters many secrets from various ministries. He spied upon political parties as well.

While rejecting his anticipatory bail application, the Delhi High Court observed, "Ramswaroop hardly had any concern or regard for India's unity, security and welfare. He was working as if he was a citizen of Taiwan though domiciled in India. He had been sending all types of information to Taiwan and other countries. It is apparent from the documents that he stole most of this information which had direct bearing on delicate matters like the nation's defence and security."

During interrogation after his arrest, Ramswaroop was made to undergo Polygraph lie-detection tests. He admitted that apart from Taiwan, he was spying for Israel, West Germany and America. During a raid on his office, it was discovered that he had earned a lot in foreign exchange. Prior to this, China had sent a protest letter to External Affairs ministry about his activities. During the raid on September 7, Ramswaroop was abroad. He was taking part in a meeting of Asian-Pacific Anti-communist League in Dallas in America. This body was supposed to be a front organisation of CIA.

Another raid was organised on 28th September at his residence and office situated at Sujan Singh Park. The officers of intelligence agencies found thirteen important files there. These files were kept in an orderly manner and had headings superscribed on them.

However, he defended the charges laid on him saying that – the information passed on to the foreign organisations was nothing more than the clippings from print media; the foreign currency found at his residence during the raid was collected by his late son who had a hobby of collecting old and foreign notes; and finally, the records and files found at his Sujan Singh Park office contained no such secret information. All that information was taken from the printed material only. None of it can be secret, he argued.

Ultimately, in the early 1990 after the new government has come to power, Ramswaroop scandal has taken a sudden twist and he was acquitted of all the charges levelled by the C.B.I.

How a Bunch of Flowers Trapped Eichmann

One of the most callous war criminals of all time was trapped by an alert spy – because of a bouquet of flowers. Ricardo Klement bought the blooms in the Suarez suburb of Buenos Aires, Argentina, on 21 March 1960. Just over two years later, he died on the gallows in Tel Aviv, Israel. For the bouquet was final proof that Klement was Adolf Eichmann, the Nazi most hated by Jews all over the world. And it ended an astonishing 15-year hunt involving the espionage organisations of three nations.

Eichmann was the SS lieutenant-colonel with overall responsibility for Hitler's extermination of 6 million Jews. At the end of the war, he destroyed his records and personal file, burned all his photographs, and disguised himself as a Luftwaffe private. American forces who arrested him in May 1945 were not too interested in ordinary airmen, and in the confusion Eichmann managed to slip out of sight – but not out of Jewish minds.

The intelligence services of the new state of Israel were at first too busy with its baptism of fire – the 1948 war of independence against Arab neighbours – to settle old scores. But in 1950, a Mossad agent in the North African port of Tangier reported that 30 high-ranking Nazi fugitives had fled Europe via Spain and Italy – and one, Ricardo Clementi, had headed for Latin America on refugee papers issued by Vatican City authorities.

Then, in 1957, a German half-Jew who settled in Argentina after going blind in Dachau concentration camp told German secret service men investigating Nazi escapes that a schoolmate of his daughter had made anti-semitic statements praising Hitler for murdering Jews. The boy's name was Nikolaus Klement. And when the girl described her father, the ex-prisoner was convinced he was Eichmann. His hunch was reported to Dr Fritz Bauer, chief prosecutor in the German state of Hesse. Dr Bauer, himself a Jew, passed the news secretly to Tel Aviv, giving the Israelis Klement's address: 4261 Chacabuco Street, Olivos, Buenos Aires.

It was confirmation of a lead Mossad had established for itself. Espionage chiefs knew Eichmann's wife Veronika, who disappeared from her home in Linz, Austria, with her two children, at Easter 1952, would have to return to Vienna to renew her passport. When she eventually turned up, Mossad men were waiting, and shadowed her day and night before losing her trail Argentina.

Israel's supreme spymaster, Isser Harel, now took charge of the Eichmann operation. His team had two priorities: to establish beyond all doubt that Klement was Eichmann – seizing the wrong man would make Israel an international laughing stock – and to do it without alerting their target, or Nazi sympathisers who might help him to escape. Delicate negotiations with the Argentinian secret service revealed that Buenos Aires knew Klement's real identity, but the authorities were prepared to let Israel deal with him quietly to avoid the embarrassment of extradition proceedings, which would disclose to the world that Argentina was knowingly harbouring war criminals.

Revenge was not the only Israeli motive. Anti-communist hysteria in America had led to a neo-Fascist backlash, and some people were already reappraising Hitler's regime, and claiming his oppression of the Jews had been exaggerated.

The world was beginning to forget. For the same reason, simple assassination of Eichmann would not do. Simon Wiesenthal, the concentration-camp survivor who had later dedicated his life to tracking down war criminals, said: 'If you kill him, the world will never learn what he did. There must be an accounting, a record for history.'

Mossad watchers in Argentina began a discreet round-the-clock surveillance of Klement and his family. Long-range photographs were sent back to Tel Aviv to be shown to death camp survivors. None could positively identify Eichmann. It had been so long ago, they had seen him only fleetingly.

The longer the watch continued, the greater became the chances of discovery by ex-Nazis or Argentinians not in the know. Then came the breakthrough. Klement was photographed buying flowers on 21 March as he left his work at the Mercedes Benz factory in Suarez. He was still carrying them when he arrived home in Olivos. One of the watchers made the vital connection between the date and the action. 21 March was Eichmann's wedding anniversary. If Klement was Mrs. Eichmann's second husband, he would hardly celebrate his predecessor's special day.

Harel now had the go-ahead to put into operation what was later described as the best-organised kidnapping ever made by a secret service. With the Argentinians agreeing to a neutral role, neither overtly helping nor hindering the operation, he hand-picked an eleven-strong team, including a doctor. Some of them made their own way to Buenos Aires by different routes, and established two safe houses, one for holding Eichmann, the other in case the first was discovered.

The rest of the team arrived in Argentina disguised as air crew on an El AI plane which flew in on 12 March 1960, carrying top Israeli diplomats to help celebrate the 150th anniversary of Argentina's independence. By that time, Eichmann was already in Israeli hands. Three agents bundled him into a car seconds after he stepped off the bus from work on the evening of May 11. He was rushed to the safe house, stripped, and examined carefully for distinguishing marks. The appendicitis scar, the scar above the left eyebrow, and the SS giveaway, the blood group tattoo under the left armpit, were all there. The spies had their man. A pre-arranged code alerted Tel Aviv to the good news.

When the El Al plane was ready to leave, Eichmann was drugged, and his guards, posing as nurses and relatives, drove him to Buenos Aires airport with forged papers allowing him to be a car crash victim with head injuries who was just fit enough to travel, but could not be disturbed. The cover worked perfectly. Within 24 hours, the man whom the Jews hated most was in Tel Aviv.

Israel was scrupulous in ensuring that the full procedure of the law was carried through, but the result of the trial, which began on 12 December 1961, was never in doubt. Eichmann was convicted of 15 charges of deporting and causing the death of millions of Jews, and being a party to the murder of thousands of gipsies and 91 children. He was hanged on 31 May, 1962.

The Traitors

The messenger who stood in front of Ivan the Terrible was trembling so much that Ivan raised his iron-pointed staff, and pinned his foot to the floor. Then he ordered him to read aloud the letter he was carrying. It was from Prince Andrei Kurbski, Ivan's greatest general. Kurbski had fled to Poland, and offered his services to Ivan's enemy, King Sigismund. In his letter, he accused the Csar of cruelty and tyranny. Ivan's response was to have Kurbski's wife and child seized and murdered. For the rest of his life "the traitor Kurbski" remained his pet hate; if he could have laid hands on him, he would have devised the lengthiest and cruellest torture he could imagine. In a famous sixty-page letter, Ivan accused Kurbski of damning his soul before God by committing treason to his sovereign.

No historian has ever blamed Kurbski. He had lost an important battle in Livonia. Ivan had accused him of cowardice and treachery before; if he had remained, he would probably have been executed. If it was treason from I van's point of view, it was common sense from Kurbski's.

This same ambiguity hangs over the whole question of treason. "Treason" implies that a man has deliberately and coldly turned traitor to someone to whom he owes allegiance. The "traitor" seldom sees it that way. Sir Thomas More disapproved of Henry the Eighth's divorce from Catherine of Aragon; the king had him executed for treason, but history has decided he is a saint. Anne Boleyn was also executed on a charge of treason—it was actually a trumped up charge of adultery, the king having got sick of her bad manners. Henry's daughter Bloody Mary (who came to the throne on the death of her half brother, Edward VI) had Lady Jane

Grey, Archbishop Cranmer and Sir Thomas Wyatt executed for treason, although Wyatt was the only one who actually took part in a rebellion. Queen Elizabeth, who came near to being another of Bloody Mary's victims, had her cousin Mary Queen of Scots executed for treason. Elizabeth's successor, James I, had Sir Walter Raleigh beheaded in 1618; the evidence against him was particularly flimsy.

In short, treason has usually been a ruler's excuse for having somebody murdered. Sometimes there was a semblance of an excuse, as in the massacres that followed Bonnie Prince Charlie's attempt to seize the throne of England, or the judicial slaughters presided over by Judge Jeffreys after Monmouth's unsuccessful rebellion. But in many cases, as the Encyclopaedia Britannica admits, "the law was considerably strained in order to ensure a conviction".

In modern times, there has been an interesting change. Treason has ceased to be merely political; it has become ideological. Sir Roger Casement did not regard himself as an Englishman; he regarded himself as an enemy of England. But the English still hanged him as a traitor. Bernard Shaw had the sense to advise Casement to make a great speech of defiance, instead of trying to defend himself. Casement rejected the advice, and he died. But when Adolf Hitler tried to overthrow the German government in his putsch of 1923, and stood trial for treason, he instinctively knew that the best method of defence was attack; he hurled a magnificent speech of defiance at the court, and as a consequence, spent only thirteen months in prison. In effect, he was arguing that treason is not treason when it is motivated by political idealism.

Almost without exception, all the "great traitors" of the twentieth century fall within this category. The major

exception is Colonel Alfred Redl, whose treason probably cost his country a quarter of a million lives. But then, Redl's country was the Austria of Franz Ferdinand, a monarch who determinedly refused to allow his nation to enter the twentieth century. It is therefore appropriate that Redl should be the last important representative of the old type of traitor.

Redl was a highly intelligent man who came from a poor family; he was also a homosexual. In the Austria of the nineteenth century, the army offered a certain mode of advancement to one of Redl's intelligence. In the early years of the century, his rise was rapid. His imagination brought him to the attention of Baron von Giesl, head of the Austro-Hungarian intelligence service; he placed the young officer in charge of espionage—hardly an important activity in that rather old-fashioned, militaristic nation. But Redl proved to be brilliant. He had the kind of imagination that would have taken him far in the C.I.A. He learned to use hidden cameras to photograph unsuspecting visitors; he coated objects with a fine dust, to get their fingerprints; he recorded their conversations (on old Edison cylinders). For the first decade of the 20th century, he was a high-powered spy.

Unfortunately, he lived in a country where homosexuality was regarded as pure, deliberate wickedness. In the drawing-rooms where the elegant and witty Colonel Redl was a welcome guest, any suspicion of his sexual tastes would have been enough to ruin him. It was necessary for him to be discreet. And, since his sexual appetite was strong, this meant that, like Oscar Wilde, he had to be prepared to pay male prostitutes. It was an expensive business.

A Russian secret agent got wind of Redl's secret. And sometime around the year 1903, he informed Redl that if he wanted to avoid scandal, it would be necessary to aid the Russian secret service in certain minor matters. No one knows the details. All that is certain is that a combination of blackmail and bribery turned Redl into a traitor.

Von Giesl moved to Prague, and Redl went with him. His place in Vienna was taken by an adoring disciple, Captain Maximilian Ronge. Ronge was not a brilliant innovator, like Redl, but he was painstaking and precise. One of Redl's ideas was the institution of strict postal censorship; Ronge made sure it was carried out thoroughly. And in 1913, in the course of routine inspection, one of his agents came across two poste restante letters, addressed simply to "Opera Ball 13". Both envelopes contained fairly large sums of money. Ronge ordered his agents to watch the post office and see who came for the envelopes. They waited for weeks in the police station next door, waiting for the ringing of a bell that would tell them that the letters were being collected. One day, it rang. They rushed next door—in time to see a taxi vanishing. They managed to trace the cab to a hotel; there they were told their quarry had taken a cab to another hotel, the Klomser. And on the cab seat, one of the agents picked up a small suede sheath, of the sort that contained nail clippers. He asked the clerk at the Klomser if he knew the owner of the sheath. The clerk took it, and approached a good looking man of military bearing. The man nodded and slipped the sheath into his pocket. It was Colonel Redl.

One agent shadowed Redl; the other telephoned Rouge. Ronge was shattered. It was impossible that the ex-head of the

Secret Service could be a traitor. He got hold of the receipts that Redl had signed to get the letters, and compared them with some of Redl's own handwriting in the files. They were identical. By this time, Redl had noticed that he was being followed. He did a stupid thing. He had some incriminating receipts in his pocket—for money from Russia. He tore these into small pieces, and cautiously scattered them as he walked. But Rouge's agents had been trained in Redl's own counterespionage methods; they collected every tiny fragment, and took them to Rouge.

Ronge went to the Commander-in-Chief of the army. He was stunned by the possibility that Redl might have been an enemy agent for years. For Austria had plans for attacking Russia and the Balkans—particularly Serbia. Redl had access to these papers—known collectively as Plan Three.

The Austrians behaved like gentlemen—which was their mistake. They called Redl at his hotel, and laid the facts before him. Redl looked pale and composed. He told them that they would find all the evidence they needed at his flat in Prague, and asked to be excused a moment. There was a shot from the next room; he had done what was expected of an officer and gentleman. Probably he didn't think too badly of himself in his last moments. He had no way of knowing that an Austrian archduke was about to be assassinated in Serbia, and that Europe would soon be at war. And it was only when that war began that the Austrian general staff found out just how far Redl had betrayed his country, and that the Serbians and Russians knew every detail of Austria's plans in advance. Redl was more than a traitor; he was the executioner of the Austro-Hungarian empire.

At the time of Redl's death, a 15-year old German boy named Ernst Wollweber, son of a Ruhr miner, was beginning to read Communist revolutionary pamphlets. Wollweber later became perhaps the greatest saboteur of all time, but he is of interest here because he was also the first of the "ideological traitors". Wollweber was a German; yet he spent his life working against Germany, for the Soviet Union. It might be objected that Wollweber was no true traitor because, like many other Germans, he fought against Hitler. But Hitler did not come to power until 1933; Wollweber was working against Germany as early as World War I, when he led a naval mutiny. Wollweber was a Communist first, a German later.

In retrospect, it seems strange that it took the western powers so long to recognise that most Communists regarded Russia as their mother country, and were therefore capable of treason. In 1941, the British Security Services committed an almost unpardonable error when they allowed a German scientist named Klaus Fuchs to sign the Official Secrets Act and gain access to secret information. Fuchs had left Germany in 1933, at the age of 22; he was not a Jew, but a Quaker—another minority persecuted by the Nazis. He was allowed to become a British citizen and work on the atomic bomb because British Security reasoned that he was more likely to give information to Russia than Germany, and in 1941 Russia was an ally anyway. From the beginning, Fuchs had no intention of observing his pledge of secrecy. He promptly contacted the Russian military attache in London and offered to pass on nuclear secrets to Moscow—for Stalin had authorised full-scale research on the atomic bomb. He collaborated closely with Russian spies in England until 1943; then he was sent to America, to work on the bomb project at Los Alamos, New Mexico. For a while, he failed to contact the American branch of the Russian espionage network, and there was a frantic effort to find him. Fuchs was enjoying the sunshine of New Mexico, and a temporary sense of freedom from anxiety. Then the Russians located him when he called on his sister in Cambridge, Mass., and once again he began passing the secrets of the atomic bomb to Russia. By this time, the English and Americans had recognised that Russia would be a rival for world power after the war, and took the most elaborate precautions to prevent Soviet scientists finding out about progress on the bomb. One single man, Klaus Fuchs, completely negated the immense security precautions of the Allies. The odd thing is that he was beginning to have pangs of conscience. Perhaps he was beginning to grow up politically. He declined to meet his contact for six months, but it made no difference; the Russians kept up a firm and gentle pressure, and eventually, Fuchs handed them the secret of the enormous advances that were being made on the atomic bomb.

In 1946, he returned to England, as the head of the theoretical division of the Atomic Energy Centre at Harwell. The Russians wanted to know about the secrets of the hydrogen bomb now, but Fuchs was unable to help. He seems to have been sick of being a spy, but there was now nothing much he could do. He went on handing over information—less valuable now—until the arrest of other spies—notably Nunn May—brought him under suspicion, and a British security agent set about the task of talking him into confessing. By this time, Fuchs was no longer at Harwell—the appointment of his father as a professor in East Germany provided an excuse for removing him. And on January 30, 1950, over a quiet lunch with the British agent, William Skardon, at an Abingdon hotel, Fuchs suddenly poured out the story of his years as a Russian catspaw. He had had enough of being a traitor. Without this confession, it is almost certain that he would never have been charged with spying. The technical charge of his trial was not treason, but spying; it lasted only ninety minutes, and Fuchs went to jail for nine years. Released in 1959, he went to West Germany and became head of the Nuclear Research Institute at Karlsruhe.

And how did Fuchs come to be suspected? Ironically, through the revelations of another traitor, this time a Russian. Igor Gouzenko was not a spy; in 1945, he was simply a clerk at the Soviet Embassy in Ottawa. Gouzenko had been brought up as a good Communist—that is, to believe that the capitalist countries enslaved their people, and hated all members of the "free" Communist world. In Canada, he was amazed to discover that the workers fared better under capitalism than he had been led to expect, and that Canadians were friendly and open. Gouzenko shrank from the prospect of a return to Moscow. He decided to defect. So, he opened the safe of the Soviet Military Attache and removed a large file. Then began a comedy of errors.

The Canadians didn't seem to want a Soviet defector. An Ottawa newspaper declined to accept the secret documents, and the Canadian police also felt this was none of their

business. The Canadian Prime Minister was contacted, and told the police to hand Gouzenko back to the Russian Embassy. Gouzenko fled back to his flat. The Russians now made their mistake—they broke his door down and tried to drag him away. In a democratic society, that is strictly against the rules; so Gouzenko was once again taken into police custody—and the Canadians slowly began to realise that they were holding the key to Russian spy rings all over the world. And spies and traitors suddenly began to pop up like worms after a shower.

There was Alan Nunn May, a British physicist who was also a Communist; he had worked in nuclear research in Ottawa, and given the Russian samples of uranium isotopes (in exchange for which he was given $200 and two bottles of whiskey). The Gouzenko papers included notes about contacting May on his return to England in 1945. And when May was arrested in 1946, the prosecution had no difficulty in proving that he had spied for the Russians; he was sentenced to ten years. His defence was that he felt it was his job as a scientist to make sure that the nuclear discoveries went to the world, not just to America—a plausible argument, and one that convinced many liberal intellectuals. No one seemed to question whether Stalin would have taken the same generous attitude if Russian scientists had been the first to discover the bomb. May was basically guilty of political naivety. The American authorities, however, took a sterner view of the matter. Gouzenko's revelations led them to Klaus Fuch's American contact, Harry Gold, who was sentenced to thirty years in jail without a trial. Gold led them to David Greenglass, an American soldier who worked at Los Alamos and who had also spied for the Russians. Greenglass saved his neck by claiming that he had been dragged into spying by pressure from his sister, Ethel Rosenberg, who, together with her husband Julius, was a devoted Communist. The Rosenbergs were sentenced to death, and in spite of a violent campaign for clemency—or perhaps because of it—the Rosenbergs went to the electric chair on June 19, 1953.

But even the atom spies were amateurs compared to the British super-traitor who is regarded as "the most important spy the Russians ever had in the West"—Kim Philby. Philby's name first came to the notice of the British public soon after the defection of the spies Burgess and Maclean in 1951. A British Member of Parliament asserted that Burgess and Maclean had been alerted a few hours before their imminent arrest by a "third man", and had made their escape to Moscow. He named this third man later—Harold

Philby, known as Kim, son of the respected Arab scholar, St. John Philby, and friend of many literary men, including poet W.H. Auden, critic Cyril Connolly, and historian Philip Toynbee.

The prime minister, Harold Macmillan, defended Philby's character. The M.P. withdrew his allegation. But Philby left his job in the Foreign Office, and became Middle East correspondent for *The Observer* and *The Economist.* Then, in January 1963, Philby vanished—and turned up again a few weeks later in Moscow, where his American-born wife later joined him. There was frantic investigation into his career. And it soon became evident that the British diplomat—and member of the British Secret Service—had been a Russian agent since the early 1930's.

Philby became a Communist at Cambridge, when he was a young man, and it was the fashionable thing to do. In Berlin and Vienna in the early 1930's, he saw Nazism at first hand, and began actively working for Communism. As a cover, Philby apparently became a Fascist sympathiser, working for an "Anglo-German Friendship" group, and later going to Spain as a journalist during the Civil War and working at Franco's headquarters. The disguise was perfect. When the Hitler war came, Philby had little trouble becoming a member of the British Secret Service. Starting in a very minor capacity, he soon demonstrated his value by putting British Intelligence in touch with a Russian spy network in Switzerland which had infiltrated the German High Command. From then on, Philby's rise was steady, until he ended as MI5's chief liaison officer with the C.I.A., with access to just about every military secret possessed by the British and Americans.

No one will ever know for certain how many secrets—atomic and otherwise Philby passed to the Russians. But the number was certainly enormous. With his old Cambridge friend, the homosexual Guy Burgess, Philby blackmailed another Foreign Office man, Donald Maclean, to join their spy network. But by 1950, both Burgess and Maclean were beginning to crack under the strain of being Russian spies, and were drinking too much and causing public scenes. MI5 became suspicious; Philby warned them, and Burgess and Maclean vanished to Moscow.

Oddly enough, this was not the end of Philby's career as a spy, even though he had been publicly named as a suspect. He went back to the Middle East as a newspaperman, and worked there for another 12 years, until 1963, before he also felt that the hounds were getting too close, and he slipped away on a Russian ship. The British Secret Service will remember him—ruefully—as one of the great arch-traitors of all time.

The meaning of treason has changed unimaginably in three or four centuries. And there is no clearer way of grasping it than to think of two names: Prince Andrei Kurbski and Kim Philby.

Bhave-Bakshi Episode

This is a case of spying for our neighbour Pakistan. Many of the people involved in this scandal had escaped the dragnet in earlier cases and continued their treacherous activities. This is the inside story of attempts made by enemy agents to find out secrets about the Indian navy.

An ambassador car was stationed on the side of the road that goes towards Jama Masjid from Chandni Chowk. The car belonged to Intelligence officers who were waiting to catch a spy. A man lay under the car posing to be doing some repairs while two sat on the back seat. Suddenly, the man sitting in the car knocked with his fingers and the man came out from under the car. He rubbed his hands and pretended to be looking for some public tap to wash them. He surveyed the goods spread by the pavement shopkeepers and the crowd going either way on the busy road. He saw a man in that crowd whom he recognised. Nodding towards the man sitting in the car, he advanced towards a water tap.

On the other side of the road, a drama was being enacted. A man collided with another man in the crowd and said, "Brother, you should look where you are going." He spoke in faultless chaste Urdu. "I am sorry, please excuse me. Some of your papers have fallen, let me retrieve them," replied the other man as he picked up an envelope from the pavement and handed it to the man who spoke in Urdu. Then, he melted into the crowd.

This drama had been enacted many times by these two men. Only this time final curtain was to be rung down. Actually, defence secrets had been passed to Pakistan in that envelope.

The intelligence officer who was washing his hands at the water tap, took out a large handkerchief from his pocket and wiped his hands. He then moved towards the man who had been given the envelope. That man was signalling for a three wheeler to stop. The intelligence officer waved the handkerchief, before he could get into the three wheeler. Within seconds, a man selling old books at the pavement and a labourer lying in a hand cart rushed towards the scooter and surrounded it. The driver of the three wheeler stood astounded when these three men surrounded the man who hailed him. In the meantime, the car also approached them and stopped near them by the side of the pavement. The man with the envelope was taken into custody at gun point. A curious crowd started to gather there and the intelligence officer calmly told them, "This man is a spy and we have arrested him."

Rajan Bakshi

The man arrested was Gul Zaman, an officer of the embassy of Pakistan. The news of his arrest was displayed in the papers of November 24. Three officers of the Pakistani embassy were declared persona non grata and asked to leave India. They were Gul Zaman, Mohammad Mushtaq and Munnavar Ali. They were suspected of spying. In retaliation, Pakistan also expelled four officers of the Indian embassy at Islamabad.

On 23rd November, Pachbhave, who worked in the photography section of the naval headquarters and an advocate Rajan Bakshi were also arrested in connection with this incident. Some secret documents pertaining to Navy were recovered from Gul Zaman on that day in Chandni Chowk. Many confidential documents were recovered from the residence of Pachbhave, when it was searched by officers of the intelligence department. He used to sell these documents to Gul Zaman. Bhave's modus operandi was quite simple. He made some extra copies of the documents given to him for copying and then smuggled them out in his tiffin box.

During investigation, it transpired that Pachbhave used to sell secret documents to the spy ring of Tika Ram, Captain Jeet Singh and Mam Chand. These people worked for Pakistan. At that time, Pachbhave worked in the Defence ministry. Somehow, he escaped detection at the time of the arrest of this gang. After some time, he re-established his contact with Pakistani spies.

Rajan Bakshi's father was commander T. Bakshi, who retired from the Indian navy. A lot of papers were seized from Bakshi's residence in Vasant Vihar. Rajan did not divulge much information to his interrogator. In 1977, a spy ring was discovered in the Planning Commission. Rajan Bakshi had defended the accused Mahabir Prasad and Natasha Reddy in that case. Natasha was a citizen of Czechoslovakia. Rajan worked as an agent for America. He maintained contacts with other countries as well. Pachbhave also spied for China apart from supplying secret documents to Pakistan.

Communist Spy: Alger Hiss

For Alger Hiss it was the second time around. Back in the summer he had undergone the ordeal of a five-week trial which ended with the jury disagreeing, eight being in favour of conviction, four against. Now, in November 1949, he faced the same ordeal all over again.

He looked older and greyer after the months of waiting, but his voice was firm as he pleaded not guilty to the two charges against him. They alleged that, giving evidence before the Red-Hunting Un-American Activities Committee, he had lied when he denied passing "classified" State Department papers to Whittaker Chambers, an admitted ex-Communist; and he had lied again in saying he had never talked with Chambers in February or March 1938.

In the normal way, he would have faced trial as a spy. Under the statute of limitations, however, he could be charged only with the lesser offence of perjury because more than three years had elapsed since the alleged events.

Hiss was 44 with a distinguished government career behind him. Apart from his work in the State Department, he had been a policy adviser to President Roosevelt at the Yalta conference, and secretary-general of the post-war United Nations conference at San Francisco. He was currently—although in a state of suspension pending the outcome of the trial—President of the Carnegie Endowment for International Peace.

Yet, at the first hearing, Chambers had claimed categorically that Hiss was a member of a Communist spy ring in Washington in the 1930's, and had refused to follow his example when, disenchanted with the Stalin purges, he quit the party.

For his part, Hiss had refused even to acknowledge that Chambers was Chambers, preferring to call him George Crosley, " A man I knew in 1933 and 1934 . . . a sort of deadbeat who purported to be a cross between Jim Tully and Jack London."

Thomas Murphy, the prosecutor, devoted much of his opening speech at the start of the second trial to Chambers, his star witness. He was an intellectual, he explained, who had become a Marxist-Leninist and a Communist agent out of fear of Hitler and men like him. "There were many people who thought that only the Russians could stop the threat of Fascism," said Mr. Murphy.

"When Chambers decided to break with the Communists," he went on, "he had to go into hiding and sleep with a gun beside him." Then, conscious of the error of his past ways, he had reemerged and started to rebuild his life, rising to be a senior editor with *Time* and *Life* magazines. "But he sometimes worked 48 hours round the clock and his health broke," said Mr. Murphy. "He then retired to become a farmer."

In August the previous year, he had testified before the Un-American Activities Committee that Hiss had been a Communist agent, but produced no documentary evidence. It was only when he repeated the charge on a radio program, and Hiss issued a libel writ, that he had lodged the documents in the case with his Baltimore lawyer.

They consisted of microfilm of State Department documents which had been hidden in a pumpkin at Chambers's Maryland farm, typed copies of State Department papers, and four memoranda in what was admittedly Hiss's own handwriting. Why had Chambers taken so long to produce them? "He just couldn't bear to go that far with his former friend," Mr. Murphy explained.

At the first trial, Hiss had been represented by Lloyd Paul Stryker, a flamboyant and dramatic courtroom operator. For the new one he had switched to Claude Cross, a big-shouldered, bullnecked lawyer from Boston with a plodding style. The main points of Cross's opening address were that Chambers, a self-confessed liar who had taken false oaths in the past to further the Communist cause, could not be believed now, and that the State papers had been leaked by someone other than Hiss.

He charged specifically that the microfilmed papers in the pumpkin had been handed to Chambers directly by Julian Wadleigh—who had already admitted acting as a Communist courier while serving in the trade agreements division of the State Department in the 1930's.

Chambers, big, ruddy-faced, the black sheep turned white, was the first prosecution witness. He admitted cheerfully his past errors—expulsion from Columbia University, where he had stolen more than 50 books from the library . . . conversion to Communism . . . editor of the Daily Worker and New Masses . . . living with a girl Party worker . . . spying.

"Hiss," he told the court, "was such an obedient Communist in 1935 that he asked the Party's permission to take a new job in the Justice Department and later in the Department of State."

Hiss had provided documents right up to April 1938. Some were microfilmed, others copy-typed by Mrs. Hiss on an old Woodstock typewriter—which now stood on a table before the jury, and was to prove one of the most critical factors in the case. Then he, Chambers, became disillusioned with what was going on inside Russia, "I considered myself a better Communist than Stalin" and he decided to abandon spying.

As late as Christmas 1938, he had come out of hiding to try to persuade Hiss to break with the Communists. "That was the last time I called on them," he said. "I feared an ambush and even thought that Hiss might assassinate me."

Nevertheless, he had stayed for dinner, and Hiss had given him a toy rolling pin as a Christmas present for his daughter. "What did you do with it?" asked Mr. Cross. "I threw it away," said Chambers. "You didn't hide it in any pumpkins, did you?" suggested the lawyer in a rare departure from his correct, plodding style.

Chambers clasped his hands together and decided to treat the sally with contempt. Judge Henry Goddard interrupted to ask: "Was that meant as a serious question?"

Cross stumbled over a few words of apology and regret. "I don't think lawyers should ask foolish questions just because some of the witness's answers may be inappropriate," said the judge. "This case will take long enough as it is."

In all, Chambers spent more than six days on the witness stand. Before he was finally allowed to step down, Murphy hammered home the point that he was a reformed character who had put his Communist treachery behind him, and who could now be relied upon to tell the truth once he had sworn on the Bible.

On re-examination Murphy asked: "On your oath and before God, Judge Goddard and this jury, did you say that Mr. Hiss passed government documents to you?"

"I did," replied Chambers firmly.

It was now time for the cool voice of bureaucracy to cast doubts on the defence claim that the four handwritten memoranda had been composed by Hiss in the course of his normal duties, and later filched by someone else.

Eunice Lincoln, secretary to Hiss in 1938 and a State Department employee for 31 years, took the stand and examined the memoranda. Her comment suggested that Hiss must have written them for some private purpose rather than as part of his job. "I cannot recall seeing anything similar to these in all my years in the State Department," she said.

It was next the turn of the Woodstock typewriter to go under the microscope. Four easels were set up in court. One held private letters and memos which Mrs. Hiss admitted typing; the second the 47 documents which Chambers had produced to his lawyer in Baltimore; the third blow-ups of the microfilmed documents hidden in the pumpkin, and the last the State Department originals.

The jury, which had flagged under the strain of listening to the cocky and self-assured Chambers for more than six days, sat up and took a new interest as Ramos Feehan, an F.B.I. typewriter expert, probed the exhibits from his special point of view. Their eyes swivelled from easel to easel as he pointed out the peculiarities of some of the type faces: a capital A, the small g, e, i, o, a, u, d, r, l.

By the time he had finished it was clear that all but one—document No. 10—of the 47 Baltimore documents had been copied on the Woodstock belonging to Mrs. Hiss. It was equally clear that, unless the defence could prove conclusively that someone other than her had actually done the typing, the chances of clearing their client were slim.

It was the defence contention that Mrs. Hiss had given the typewriter to the Catletts, the family of her Negro maid, and that it was no longer in her possession at the material time. The second part of that claim took a denting when one of the Catlett boys said in the witness box that he could remember exactly when the typewriter came into the family.

"It was not later than 1936," he said. "It was the day we moved into a new house and had the electricity turned on. Up to then we'd had kerosene lamps. I'll never forget the day when we could afford to have the electricity turned on."

Mr. Murphy slapped into evidence a document from the power company. It showed the family had moved into their new home and had the electricity switched on not in 1936, but on January 17, 1938, a date uncomfortably late for Alger Hiss.

The traitorous Wadleigh, blinking behind thick glasses, denied that any of the 500 or so documents he had passed to Chambers in his years as a courier were among the evidence in court. Finally, on the 16th day, the prosecution rested its case—but only after calling the explosive testimony of Mrs. Hede Massing, a former Viennese actress.

They had failed to win the right for her to give testimony at the first trial. Now, after several objections from Mr. Cross, she described how she had been an active Communist agent from the end of 1933 to 1937, and how Hiss had tried to lure into his "cell" one of her workers – Noel Field, a former State Department employee, who had fled with his wife behind the Iron Curtain just a few months before the trial.

In a conversation at Field's home, she recalled, "I said to Mr. Hiss: 'I understand you are trying to get Noel Field away from my organisation and into yours.' He said: 'So you are this famous girl who is trying to keep Noel Field away from me.' And I said: 'Yes.' And he said, as far as I can remember: 'Well, we will see who is going to win.' At which point I said: 'Well, you realise you are competing with a woman.'

After that, one of them—she couldn't be sure which one—had commented: "Whoever is going to win, we are both working for the same boss."

The trial continued in a curious atmosphere on December 22, the last day before the court closed for the Christmas recess. Judge Goddard insisted on having the windows open, and Mr. Cross proceeded with his attempt to save Hiss to the sound of carols and sleigh-bells.

By the end of the day, he had managed to cast doubts on certain details of the friendship between Hiss and Chambers, and to discredit to a large degree the prosecution's claim that, in November 1937, they were on such close terms that Hiss had given Chambers a $400 loan to buy a car.

The real assault, however, began when the court resumed on January 6, and Judge Goddard allowed—for the first time in Federal Courts—psychiatric testimony in an attempt to discredit a witness. The two men brought in to attack the personality of Chambers were Dr. Carl Binger, a distinguished, athletic-looking psychiatrist, and Dr. Henry Murray, former director of the Harvard Psychological Clinic.

Dr. Binger, who had heard much of Chambers' testimony, and had studied all his stories, poems, articles, and translations, said he was "suffering from a condition known as psychopathic personality, a disorder of the character whose distinguishing features are amoral and a social."

Such people, he explained, did not take into account the ordinary accepted conventions of morality and had "no regard for the good of society and of individuals". Consequently, they were often destructive of both. Some symptoms of the condition, he went on, were "chronic, persistent and repetitive lying; acts of deception and misrepresentation; alcoholism and drug addiction; abnormal sexuality, vagabondage, begging, inability to form stable attachments and a tendency to make false accusations."

Dr. Murray said his speciality had been the analysis of psychopathic personalities through the internal evidence of their writings. What did he think of the writings of Whittaker Chambers? "I have found," he stated, "a higher proportion of images of disintegration and destruction, filth and dirt, decay and decomposition and death than in any writings I have ever examined."

Juries are notoriously prone to be irritated by the claims of psychiatrists and psychologists to know what really makes people tick. Any prejudices the Hiss jury may have had in this direction were well bolstered by the prosecutor's masterly handling of the two experts, and of Dr. Binger in particular.

Mr. Murphy, slipping easily into the role of a plain homespun kind of fellow not to be bamboozled by highfalutin nonsense about the roots of personality, took Dr. Binger up on his statement that "personal untidiness and bad teeth are symptoms of the psychopath".

"But, doctor," he inquired genially, "how about dear old Will Rogers, and Owen D. Young, and Bing Crosby? They were no fashion plates. Were they psychopathic?"

"Not on that evidence," replied the witness.

"You say normal people hide things in banks," Mr. Murphy went on. "How about the mother of Moses? Didn't she hide him in the bullrushes?"

"She could hardly have put him in a safe-deposit box," retorted Dr. Binger in his only snappy answer of the day.

They also had a brisk exchange on whether Dr. Binger's conclusions from studying Chambers' testimony and writings were necessarily the only ones that could be drawn. "Doctor," the lawyer asked in the course of his painstaking attack, "would you say that other psychiatrists, let us say as qualified as yourself, might perhaps have a different opinion based upon the facts you have?"

"I should be very surprised if they did." "Apart from your surprise, would a difference of opinion be possible?" "Naturally it would be." "Doctors have been known to disagree frequently on diagnosis?" "Frequently." "And some doctors have been known to be wrong on diagnosis?" "Frequently." "Have you ever been wrong?" Mr. Murphy asked bluntly.

"Certainly," Dr. Binger confessed.

The final speech for the defence began on January 19 when the trial was in its tenth drawn-out week. Cross's basic case was that Chambers was a chronic liar, and that the alleged corroboration was "pure fabrication". He emphasised the case of Baltimore No. 10, the document which the F.B.I. expert established had not been typed on Mrs. Hiss's Woodstock typewriter.

"Chambers had taken his oath here that all the documents came from Alger Hiss alone, and then, under cross-examination, when I took out Baltimore 10 and laid it on the jury rail, he swore with equal solemnity that it might have come from another man."

Chambers and his wife—who had also given evidence—had been unable to agree on the precise facts about any of the supposed visits between the two families. Mr. Cross also tried to show that only three of the microfilm documents had even been in Hiss's hands. Subsequently, he claimed, Wadleigh had stolen the documents and passed them on to Chambers. All the typewritten documents had been stolen by an unknown confederate of Chambers in the Far Eastern Division of the State Department.

And where did the Woodstock typewriter come in? Mr. Cross stuck to his claim that it had not been in Mrs. Hiss's possession during the critical period. He suggested that an accomplice, perhaps posing as a Woodstock repair man, might have been able to purloin it for a time from the Catlett household and make use of it.

When he had his last say for the prosecution, Mr. Murphy dismissed this final suggestion with one word: "Pah!" He also jeered at the defence's introduction of the fact that Hiss had campaigned hard at the State Department in 1939 to get the Neutrality Act amended in favour of the Allies.

"Why did he do that?" asked Mr. Murphy. "Why, he did it because, when Chambers quit the Party, Hiss became the hottest thing in Washington. He had to take the opposite position. He had to be a good boy from then on."

He then returned to the subject of the typewriter. "You heard Perry Catlett say he took it to a typewriter repair shop as soon as he got it," Mr. Murphy pointed out. "We show him that that shop did not open until September 1938. All right, we say, maybe another place. Yes, he thinks it is. We then prove that that one didn't open until May, 1938.

"Isn't it the truth that the Catletts got that typewriter when Chambers quit the Communist Party – in April 1938?"

The prosecutor also drew the jury's attention to typing errors—as opposed to flaws in the type faces—that were common both to Mrs. Hiss's private letters and memos, and the copied State Department documents. He advised them when they got into the jury room to "look for an R done for an I, a 0 for a I, a F for a G and an F for a D".

He pointed to the typewriter and the documents on the table before the jury. "The documents are the golden calf," he said. "Each of them has a message. What is it? Alger Hiss was a traitor."

It was the typewriter that proved to be the deciding factor. After an absence of two-and-a-half hours, the jury returned to ask if they could have read to them the evidence about when the Catletts got the machine, when Mrs. Hiss said she had disposed of it, and also the evidence about the typewritten documents.

Then, after being out for nearly 24 hours, they found the accused guilty on both counts. Hiss paled, swallowed slightly, but still held his head high as the verdict was announced and he heard the sentence: five years' imprisonment.

Mr. Murphy asked for Hiss to be committed to jail "as all convicted defendants ought to be". Judge Goddard looked up. "I think not, Mr. Murphy," he said mildly. Hiss, who had behaved honourably while awaiting both his first and second trials, was released on $5000 bail pending appeal.

But first Judge Goddard allowed him to make a statement to the court. "I would like to thank your Honour for the Opportunity again to deny the charges that have been made against me. I want only to add that I am confident that, in the future, the full facts of how Whittaker Chambers was able to carry out forgery by typewriter will be disclosed."

Hiss went to jail in 1951. He went on to serve 44 months of his five year sentence, and ever since his release has continued to protest his innocence. In 1983, the Supreme Court refused a third formal request to set aside the 1950 perjury conviction. Alger Hiss argues that recent documentary evidence shows misconduct by the government prosecutors. His lawyer stated at the most recent Supreme Court appearance, "The case is still an unhealed wound in the nation's body politic."

The Spy Masters

The corpse that was dragged out of the icy waters of the Baltic Sea was still clutching two hefty books in its arms. The Russian captain of the vessel which found him was puzzled; why on earth should a sailor want to leap into the sea holding heavy books—and why hadn't he let go of them when he was drowning? The Russian was a novice in modern warfare; it was only September, 1914, and most naval and military men were still naive enough to believe that wars were fought only with soldiers. They knew little about spies and secret codes.

The captain's superiors in the Russian Admiralty were not much wiser. They recognised that they had captured German code books—handed by the captain of the sinking Magdeburg to one of his men, with orders to drop them into the sea. But it did not strike them as a particularly exciting discovery. A few days later, the Russian attache in London called on Winston Churchill, the First Lord of the Admiralty, and told him that they had found the German naval code books. If the English would care to send a ship, they were welcome to them.

Churchill immediately appreciated their value. He sent the ship, and rushed the books to Admiral Oliver, head of Intelligence. Oliver handed them to one of his best men, an ex-teacher named Alfred Ewing. Ewing knew all about codes: he had been trying to crack the German naval code for months.

He grabbed the latest batch of coded messages, picked up from radio signals sent out from the German naval base at Wilhelmshaven. Within a few minutes, he knew that fortune had presented him with a prize. It was possible for him to read the secret orders of Grand Admiral Tirpitz and other senior commanders.

Two months later, in November 1914, Ewing was given a new boss – Captain William Reginald Hall, known as "Blinker" (because of a twitching eyelid). The new head of Naval Intelligence did not look in the least like a spy; he was short, rotund, and cheerful. In fact, he was one of the most brilliant spymasters in the history of espionage.

The first thing Hall wanted to know was whether the codes could tell them something useful. On December 14, 1914, Ewing decoded a report that announced that the German fleet intended to sail. Quietly, Hall moved his own ships into position in the North Sea. Two days later, Britain suffered its first naval bombardment, as ships of the German navy pounded the north-east coastal towns of Scarborough and Hartlepool with their heavy guns. Hall signalled his own battle cruisers, lying nearby, and told them to move in for the kill.

All day, Churchill and Hall waited tensely for news. When it came, it was disappointing. Fog and rain had swept down over the North Sea as the British navy moved in. There had been a few shots exchanged, and the Germans had vanished into the mist. Churchill was disappointed; but to his surprise, Hall was looking jubilant. "There'll be a next time!" he cried. But that stoical reaction hardly explained his delight. He had been struck by a kind of vision. Modern warfare depended on surprise. The Germans had gained the element of surprise when they invaded Belgium. But ever since Marconi's discovery of radio in the 1890s, the surprise depended on a man with a transmitter and a code book. If he could find all the code books, it would be possible to anticipate every important move of the enemy. But how was he to do this? The two he had were important, but they were not the only ones.

For example, there were the strange signals coming from a transmitter in Brussels. Ewing had been working on the code for months, without success; Hall had a feeling, it concealed important secrets. He ordered his spies to find out everything they could about the Brussels transmitter. This was not difficult; it had been there, in an office in the Rue de Loi, before the war. More inquiries revealed that it was operated by a young man called Alexander Szek. "That name doesn't sound German," said Hall thoughtfully.

He made more inquiries—and suddenly knew that he was close to a solution. Alexander Szek, he discovered, was an Austro-Hungarian subject who had been born in Croydon, in south London. Members of his family were still living in England. Hall persuaded Szek's father to write Alexander a letter, begging him to work for the British. A British agent in Holland smuggled it to Brussels and soon discovered that Szek was not particularly pro-German. The Germans had persuaded him to work for them because he was a good radio engineer. But neither was he a born spy; the idea of stealing the German secret code terrified him. The British hinted that his family in England might be put in prison if he refused; so, finally, Szek agreed.

Szek was not himself in possession of the code; a German Intelligence officer worked with him, and showed it to him when he needed it. But he could memorise it—a few figures at a time—and write it out.

In the early months of 1915, Szek began stealing the code. Every time he completed a page, he handed it over to the British agent. His nerve, however, was beginning to crack. He told the agent that he wanted to be smuggled to England as soon as he had finished copying the code. The agent pointed out that if he did that, the Germans would immediately change the cipher. But Szek was insistent.

Then, a short while afterwards, Szek was found dead in his room in Brussels. He appeared to have been killed by a burglar. The British later said he was a victim of the Germans. The truth, almost certainly, is that he was murdered by the British. Next, to their horror, the Germans suddenly discovered that their "surprise" moves were no longer surprises. Their European armies found they were being outgeneralled because the enemy was able to anticipate their moves. The day of modern espionage, the espionage of the "cold war", had arrived.

During the American War of Independence, there were some notable espionage exploits. Nathan Hale, spying for the Americans, was captured and executed in the first year of the hostilities. He died saying, "I only regret that I have but one life to lose for my country"—the kind of sentiment that would make a modern spy snort cynically. Hale became a martyr; so did the British spy, Major John Andre, who liaised with the infamous traitor Benedict Arnold. Women spies also came into their own during the war—since no one could tell which side a woman belonged to, and the officers of both nations were far too gallant to search one of the "gentle sex".

Belle Boyd, a "rebel" spy, had Northern officers quartered in her house in Martinsburg, Virginia. She was thus able to gather all kinds of information about troop movements, which she promptly relayed to General Stonewall Jackson. (On one famous occasion, she got through the Northern lines and delivered a message that enabled Jackson to win a battle.)

The most amusing thing about her career is that the Northern officers were soon convinced she was a spy, but were forbidden by chivalry to take any action. She was finally arrested, when one of her dispatches fell into the hands of a Union agent— but she was exchanged for a Northern prisoner, and became a heroine in the South. The careers of "Rebel Rose" Greenhow and Pauline Cushman (a spy for the North) were equally remarkable, and now belong to American folklore.

But it was under the Soviet regime that spying became the major industry we know today. The Russians always had their tradition of secret police; under the last of the Czars, it was called the Ochrana, and its chief business was to root out revolutionary activity. Trotsky's secret police, the "Cheka", soon became the dreaded G.P.U. But after Lenin's death, the congenitally suspicious Stalin felt uneasy about the increasing power of the secret police. Its head, Yagoda, was executed in the purges of 1937. It was fortunate for the Russian Intelligence Service that two of its greatest spies, Ernst Wollweber and Richard Sorge were working abroad, out of Stalin's reach.

It is generally agreed by experts that Sorge was probably the greatest spy of all time. Born in Russia in 1895, his family moved to Germany when he was a child. As a student he became passionately left wing; he joined the German

Communist Party, and eventually became its intelligence chief. He trained in Russia, then moved around Europe, building up spy rings in Scandinavia and Britain. (The British Secret Service spotted him fairly quickly; after that Sorge always maintained that it was one of the best in the world.)

In Russia in the late twenties, he was involved in clashes between the Army Secret Service and the Secret Police (G.B.), and his fate might well have been the same as that of Yagoda. Fortunately for him, the Communists decided that he would be useful in the far East, specifically Japan. His instructions were simple, the Soviets were firmly convinced that the great threats of the future would come from Germany and Japan.

He was well qualified for the job. A highly intelligent man, who spoke several languages, he also had the perfect cover. He was an ardent womaniser. With so many shreds of scandal attached to his name, and a reputation for being an incorrigible philanderer, who could believe that he was also a spy and a top level Communist official? He didn't seem to be serious enough.

Nevertheless, in Japan, Sorge began to recruit agents. These included Agnes Smedley, a well-known author of books on China, and a friend of Mao Tse-Tung; Ozaki, a Japanese correspondent; a Yugoslav pressman, Voukelitch. Methodically, Sorge also built up an intelligence network in China. Then, when Hitler came to power in 1933, he was given another task: to spy on the Germans Japan. There was one important preliminary—he had to apply for membership of

the newly-formed Nazi Party. Hitler's Intelligence system was so inadequate that Sorge was given a party card. Back in Tokyo, he then completed his own Japanese spy network with the addition of an American-Japanese. Miyagi Yotuka. Miyagi and Ozaki were ordered to form their own sub-network of Japanese spies.

Sorge's charm—and his cover as a correspondent for the *Frankfurt Times*—soon made him friends at the German embassy, among them a military attaché, Lieut-Colonel Eugen Ott. Meanwhile Ozaki became a leading member of a "breakfast club" of Japanese intellectuals, with close connections with the cabinet. It was he who told Sorge in advance of Japan's projected attack on China: information which delighted the Kremlin, because while Japan was fighting China; it was unlikely to invade Russia.

Later, when Colonel Ott was appointed German ambassador, Sorge had sources of information about German and Japanese policies which made him the most important secret agent in the world. Sorge knew about the Japanese attack on Pearl Harbour—in December 1941—weeks before it happened. He knew the exact date when the Germans intended to invade Russia, and if it had not been for Stalin's complacency in ignoring his information, "Operation Barbarossa" would have been defeated within days.

The head of Japanese Intelligence, Colonel Osaki (not to be confused with the agent, Ozaki), knew there was a major spy network in Japan; his radio receivers picked up their coded messages, but he could not read them. Finally, he became convinced that Sorge was his man. He asked a German attache to arrange a meeting with Sorge at a nightclub. Over a bottle of sake, he told Sorge about a beautiful girl who danced in the cabaret—about how many men were in love with her. Sorge was curious and his curiosity was increased by the mask the girl wore. He began to spend every evening at the club, until finally the girl became his mistress. But she was an agent of Colonel Osaki's—an aristocratic Japanese girl who had been asked to sacrifice her self-respect for her country.

One night while driving her home, Sorge stopped his car, and started to make love to the girl. Then he asked her to come back and spend the night with him. Before deciding the dancer asked him for a cigarette. Sorge took out his case—and a tiny roll of paper fell from it. He carefully tore the paper up, and threw the pieces out of the window. The girl made an excuse to get to a telephone, and rang Japanese Intelligence. Almost as soon as the car had driven away, Japanese agents were collecting the torn fragments of paper. The next morning, as Sorge lay asleep beside the girl, Colonel Osaki walked into the bedroom. He handed Sorge a section of the message he thought he had destroyed. The spy stood up and bowed. He knew he was defeated.

According to one account, Sorge faced his executioners—in November 1944—with complete nonchalance, smoking a cigarette. But there is no definite evidence that Sorge was executed. It is known that he claimed a reprieve on the grounds that he was a Soviet citizen, and that Russia was not at war with Japan. A British diplomat who knew Sorge claimed that he saw him in Shanghai in 1947. And it was at about this time that the girl who had betrayed Sorge was murdered. So it seems possible that he ended his days behind a desk in the G.P.U. headquarters in Moscow.

After the war, Soviet Intelligence suffered a heavy blow when the attache Gouzenko defected to the West, and took with him a complete list of Russian spies and their contacts. The result was that Russia decided to reorganise her spy system in the United States. The man who was chosen for the job was Colonel Rudolph Abel.

Abel was, in fact, already in New York when Gouzenko's defection led to the arrest of the Rosenbergs and the rest of their network. He had been a veteran of the secret service ever since Trotsky had founded it after the 1917 Revolution. Now, in 1948, on the collapse of the Soviet spy network in America, Abel patiently set about rebuilding it.

The master spy established himself in an artist's studio in Fulton Street, Brooklyn. On the door was a notice: Emil Goldfus, Photographer. As well as film and cameras, the place was also full of radio equipment—Abel explained that he was a radio enthusiast, and supplemented his income repairing sets, which was true. His cover, like Sorge's, was almost perfect. A good-looking, intelligent, middle-aged man, he liked girls, played the guitar well, and was a more than passable painter. The artists who attended parties in his studio regarded him as a typical Bohemian with typical artistic activities.

In fact, he was busy contacting the remnants of Russia's spy ring in the United States, and putting them to work again. He also re-contacted various American embassy officials who had been blackmailed into aiding Russian Intelligence when they were stationed in Moscow. By 1953, the revitalised Russian spy ring was stronger than ever. The secrets that flowed to Moscow via Abel's transmitter included details of the American hydrogen bomb and atomic submarines.

His downfall was a new assistant, Reino Hayhanen, a Russian Finn. Like many Finns, he was a heavy drinker. He was also unhappy about spying in a foreign country. Abel had Hayhanen's wife sent out to join him, but this proved to be a mistake. The couple quarrelled all the time, and Hayhanen became less efficient than ever. He resented his lack of contact with Abel; their meetings were often in public parks, or in the New York subway.

In 1955, Abel went to Russia; when he returned, he discovered that Hayhanen had been drunk for weeks. He told his demoralised assistant that it was time he journeyed to Russia for a holiday. Hayhanen was terrified; with his reputation as a drunk, it was a 50/50 chance that he would be eliminated. He travelled as far as Paris—then went to the American embassy, and explained that he wanted to defect. So, one more Russian spy network collapsed. Abel was sentenced to 30 years in jail; but he spent only five there. In 1962, he was exchanged for the American pilot, Gary Powers. And Russia's greatest spy since Sorge returned after all to end his days in Moscow.

More and more the spy lives in a limbo between his employers and those whom he seeks to betray. In some cases, when the agent plays a double, or even treble, role—his life span can be calculated in terms of days rather than weeks, weeks rather than months. Ultimately, the spy finds himself with only one person left whom he can trust – himself. And when his own self-trust evaporates—as it eventually does —then he is as good as dead.

Burgess and Maclean: The Old School Spies

On the morning of May 25, 1951, diplomat Guy Burgess sat in his New Bond Street flat reading the *London Times.* He was in no hurry. A friend of his, a male dancer in a West End musical comedy, had just left, and an apparently uneventful day stretched before Burgess.

He did not have to report to the Foreign Office because he was under suspension after being sent home from his job at the British embassy in Washington. The complaints against him ranged from homosexual affairs to driving offences, from repeated drunkenness to "inattention to duty".

At 40, his career as a diplomat was clearly near its end. The Old Etonian, very much in favour of taking life as it came, was not particularly worried. Apart from *The Times,* his only immediate concern was the holiday he planned to take with a young American friend he had met on the Queen Mary, a month earlier during his voyage home in disgrace. They were due to sail from Southampton at midnight aboard the steamer Falaise, bound for Brittany.

On that same morning, another diplomat, Donald Maclean, was working away busily at his "American desk" at the

Foreign Office. It was his 38th birthday and he was in good spirits. His wife, Melinda, was expecting a baby; he had recovered from his homosexual infatuation with a Negro porter at a Soho nightspot, who had repaid his devotion by beating him up; he was looking forward to a birthday lunch with a few friends.

Then came the tip-off that changed everything. The source was a third "diplomat", Kim Philby. Philby worked ostensibly as a first secretary at the Washington embassy. In fact, he was the liaison officer between the British S.I.S. (Secret Intelligence Service) and its American counterpart, the C.I.A. (Central Intelligence Agency). He was also, like Burgess and Maclean, a Soviet agent.

Security men, trying to track down a whole series of atomic secret leakages, had suspected Maclean for some time. Now they were about to pounce, and because of his job at the very heart of Anglo-American Intelligence, Philby had been informed.

His message to Burgess was short and crisp: "Warn Donald he is about to be interrogated." Burgess, although not directly under suspicion himself, panicked. He decided not merely to warn Maclean and help him to flee the country. He would flee himself as well.

One of his first steps was to arrange an assignation with the young American due to join him on a holiday that night, and explain that the trip would have to be called off. "A friend of mine at the Foreign Office is in serious trouble," he said at their meeting in Green Park. It must have sounded a reasonable excuse. But, for once, Burgess was speaking the truth.

What had promised to be an uneventful day proved to be a busy one. Burgess hired a car "for about ten days", invested in a new suitcase and some clothes, packed, and in the early evening, climbed into the car and set out to drive to Maclean's country home at Tatsfield in Kent.

Maclean, shadowed by security men who had had him under surveillance for some weeks, caught his usual train home, the 5.19 from Charing Cross Station. It was to be for the last time. As soon as Burgess arrived with news of his impending interrogation, Maclean also packed his bags. Then, after a hasty dinner, the two spies drove down to Southampton.

They arrived only minutes before the Falaise was due to sail, abandoned the hired car on the quayside, and rushed for the gangway. "Hey," shouted a sailor, "what about the car?" "Back on Monday," called out Burgess as he boarded the cross-channel steamer—but neither he nor Maclean would ever see England again.

By a secret route they made their way to Moscow while behind them the storm broke—not only over their escape, but over the fact that two men of such unstable character had been able to betray their country over such a long period without detection.

Burgess was a talkative, once handsome but now bloated, figure who breakfasted off benzedrine tablets washed down with brandy and port, and who never tired of boasting about his sexual excesses. "I could never travel by train," he once announced at a party. "I would feel obliged to seduce the engine driver."

His Communist sympathies, like those of Maclean and Philby, went back to Cambridge—where all three had been contemporaries in the early 1930s. As an undergraduate, Burgess far outshone his two friends and "fellow-travellers". He has been described as "the most brilliant young talent of his day".

That promise was never fulfilled. He drifted from job to job, served for a brief period in the war in a minor Intelligence job, worked for the B.B.C., then finally found a niche in the Foreign Office. That he survived there from the end of the war until 1951—despite his drinking, homosexual exploits, and lack of enthusiasm for work—is a tribute to the strength of the "old school tie network".

As a spy, as in everything else, Burgess was something of a dilettante—more interested in being able to boast to his intimates that he was "working for the Reds" than actually providing his Moscow masters with information of genuine value. It is doubtful if he told them anything that changed the course of history. Maclean, however, was an entirely different prospect.

He was the son of Sir Donald Maclean, a staunch Presbyterian who had been Minister of Education under Liberal Prime Minister Herbert Henry Asquith. By the time Maclean arrived at Trinity Hall, Cambridge, to read modern languages, he was as staunch an atheist and Communist as his father was a Christian.

Outside of his studies, Maclean's main —in fact, almost sole—interest was undergraduate journalism, which he used to popularise Marxism. He had quite clearly accepted the whole Communist philosophy. It was therefore a surprise to his friends when he announced that he proposed to seek a career in the British Foreign Office—the very anthesis of Red belief.

"I have decided to join the oppressors instead of the oppressed," Maclean uttered. It was an uncharacteristically flip explanation which, along with his uncompromisingly Left-wing written views, should have aroused suspicion.

As it was, the Foreign Office accepted Maclean as a more than passable recruit. If the pro-Communist sympathies he had shown in the past were considered at all, they were dismissed as the not-uncommon excesses of an intellectual undergraduate. It did not occur to anyone in authority that he was already a committed Soviet agent.

Luck was to prove unusually kind to Maclean in his role as a spy. He was posted in the spring of 1944 to Washington as a First Secretary. With him went his wife, Melinda. The fact that he was only 31—unusually young for such a job—is an indication of the esteem in which he was held at the Foreign Office—who regarded him as one of the brightest of their bright young men.

It was only natural, when the post became vacant a couple of years later, that Maclean should be appointed British Secretary to the Combined Policy Committee on atomic affairs. The function of the Committee was to control the exchange of information on atomic matters between the United States, Canada and Britain.

This post not only enabled him to pass on to the Soviet Union details of vital atomic secrets being pooled between the countries—he was able to lay his hands on even more important information held back by the United States for security reasons.

This came about because he managed, as part of his duties, to obtain a non-escort pass to the U.S. Atomic H.Q. in Washington. He made frequent use of the privilege—usually at night when the building was more or less deserted.

Nobody knows, or is ever likely to know, exactly how much information he managed to filch on these nocturnal visits. One secret—at a time when uranium was believed to be in critically short supply—was almost certainly a cheap

American process for converting waste from South African goldmines into high-grade uranium.

Eventually, a security officer, Brian La Plante, became suspicious of the frequency with which Maclean made use of his non-escort facility and the unusual hours he kept. "I reported him and the pass was withdrawn," said La Plante. But by then the damage had been done and, with no follow-up investigation, Maclean was able to move on to his next coup.

From his privileged position he was able to monitor for his Russian task masters the top secret negotiations which led up to the signing of the Western defensive alliance—the North Atlantic Pact—in April 1949. During the negotiations, Maclean was switched to a new post, Head of Chancery at the Cairo embassy. It did not affect his efficiency as a spy because, as a Grade A embassy, Cairo was kept informed as a matter of routine about all details of British Middle East policy.

There were signs, however, that he was beginning to feel the strain of his dual role. In Washington, he had already started to drink heavily. In Cairo he drank even more, and his conduct became increasingly bizarre.

After one alcoholic binge, he broke into the apartment belonging to the United States ambassador's secretary, smashed up the furniture, stuffed some of her clothing down the lavatory, and shattered the bath with a marble shelf.

Finally, on May 11, 1950, he was sent home. Melinda had complained to the British ambassador, Sir Ronald Campbell, that it was no longer possible to control him. The official reason for his return—not far from the truth—was "a nervous breakdown".

Back in London, Maclean was given six months' leave on condition that he underwent psychiatric treatment. It was at this time, urged on by his woman psychiatrist to face up to his latent homosexuality, that Maclean embarked on his affair with the Negro porter of a Soho nightclub.

Intermittently, he still drank heavily, and friends would sometimes find him reeling about in the bar of a West club declaiming: "I am the English Alger Hiss"—a reference to the respected American State Department employee who had turned out to be a Soviet spy.

His friends did not for a moment believe that he was speaking the literal truth. They simply dismissed his mumblings as the ravings of a drunk. Maclean then returned to the Foreign Office in November, 1950. Fortune—or official naivete—continued to smile upon his spying activities. He was next appointed head of the American Department.

In his new position, Maclean was able to keep Moscow abreast of all the vital details of such matters as the U.S.-Japan Peace Treaty negotiations, and the Korean war strategy. For instance, it was through the services of Maclean that the Chinese learned—via Moscow—that President Truman had ordered General MacArthur not to retaliate even if China invaded Korea from the north.

But, although Melinda had by now returned to him, and they had bought a country house in Kent, his inner life was far from well. He still found his burden of guilt difficult to bear. By the beginning of 1951, he was again on the bottle. At times, it seemed as if he was almost seeking discovery so that he might have some peace of mind and conscience.

In one of his drinking bouts, he asked Mark Culme-Seymour, a friend from prewar days: "What would you do if I said I was working for Uncle Joe?" Culme-Seymour debated with himself whether to report the conversation, but eventually decided—as had the friends whom Maclean had told he was "an Alger Hiss"—that it was merely the eccentric remark of a man who was overimbibing.

However, the net was beginning to be drawn in on Maclean. The earlier leakages of atomic secrets were known, and for two years British security men had been trying to track down the informer. The finger pointed to Maclean even at the time when he was in London on his six months' leave for psychiatric treatment.

Then, at a three-cornered meeting of MI5, S.I.S., and Foreign Office executives, it was decided that the time was ripe to spring the trap. The next day, a Friday, the Foreign Secretary, Herbert Morrison, gave the authority for Maclean to be interrogated. The investigation would begin on the Monday. MI5 ordered their top man, William Skardon, the ex-Murder Squad detective who had unmasked atom bomb spy Klaus Fuchs, to stand by.

Then onto the scene stepped Kim Philby, "The Third Man" in Washington. It was to prove a personal tragedy for him that Burgess—the go-between in warning Maclean—should have chosen this moment to make his unnecessary flight. Had he stayed put, Philby might have continued undetected for many more years as a Soviet agent.

In the quest for the man who had tipped off Maclean, he would have figured as just one of several possible names.

But in lists drawn up of Maclean suspects and Burgess suspects, he was the only person to figure on both of them. Philby was recalled from Washington, where the Americans had made it clear that they would no longer work with him and asked to resign.

In his time as a spy, Philby had probably done even more than Maclean to damage the interests of the United States and her Western allies. He had occupied two offices of supreme trust which had put him in an ideal position from which to serve the Communist cause.

One was when—at a time that the war had not yet ended, and Russia was still officially an Anglo-American ally—he was given the task of setting up a new Soviet counterespionage section of S.I.S. The other was his key position as liaison officer between S.I.S. and the C.I.A.

No one was certain how many Western agents as well as Western secrets he betrayed. Certainly the blood of 150 Albanians was on his hands. They were men who took part, in 1950, in an American and British inspired attempt—at the height of the Cold War—to overthrow Russian influence in Albania through guerilla-fomented uprisings. But when the guerillas crossed the frontier the Russians were primed and waiting for them.

Yet Philby's treacherous career was a long time in dying. He managed to bluff his way through his interrogation on his return from Washington. As late as 1955, he was publicly cleared of being "The Third Man" by Foreign Secretary Harold Macmillan in the House of Commons. Afterwards, smiling and confident, he held a press conference. Some of the questions and answers at it were:

"If there was a third man, were you, in fact, the third man?"

"No, I was not."

"The Foreign Secretary said in the past that you had Communist associations. Is that why you were asked to resign?"

"I was asked to resign because of an imprudent association."

"That it is your association with Burgess?"

"Correct."

"What about the alleged Communist associations?"

"The last time I spoke to a Communist, knowing him to be a Communist, was sometime in 1934."

"That rather implies that you have also spoken to Communists unknowingly and now know about it?"

"Well, I spoke to Burgess last in April or May, 1951."

"He gave you no idea that he was a Communist at all?"

"Never."

Philby then went on to work as a S.I.S. secret agent in the field—his final posting being to Beirut, Lebanon, where his cover was foreign correspondent for the *Sunday Observer*. Meanwhile, back in London, irrefutable evidence was gradually being assembled of his long connection with Communism. And the fact that he had been "The Third Man" in the Burgess-Maclean affair.

At the end of 1962, S.I.S. confronted him in Beirut. He was given the choice: come home to Britain and face trial, or disappear for good behind the Iron Curtain. The British government hoped he would choose the second alternative—thus saving the "dirt" a trial would bring to light, and the inevitable demands for an inquiry into the Security Services.

Philby plumped for the Iron Curtain and fled "in secret" to Moscow. From there —speaking for himself and Burgess and Maclean—he wrote to a friend in England: "My tongue is looser now!"

Burgess and Maclean settled in Moscow after their flight and continued to serve the Russians in minor advisory roles connected with propaganda. Maclean was joined by his wife, Melinda, and their two sons.

Although the Macleans lived discreetly. Burgess still drank heavily and went on with his homosexual affairs. Western correspondents would often encounter him, usually the worse for alcohol, in Moscow hotels. He died in 1963, a few months after Philby's defection, of advanced hardening of the arteries. Before his death, he added a codicil to his will, leaving a third of his estate to Philby.

Philby, with his enormous memory for facts and faces, remained an important member of Russian Intelligence. He also helped Russian agent Gordon Lonsdale, the key figure in the Portland (a top secret underwater naval base in Dorset, England) Spy Case, to write his memoirs. Later, Philby fell in love with Melinda Maclean whom he married.

Julius and Ethel Rosenberg: Traitors or Victims?

The trial which began on March 5, 1951, in the Federal Court House in Foley Square, New York City, may well prove to be the most celebrated espionage trial in American history. Certainly no case of its kind in the United States has had wider ramifications and repercussions, both nationally and internationally.

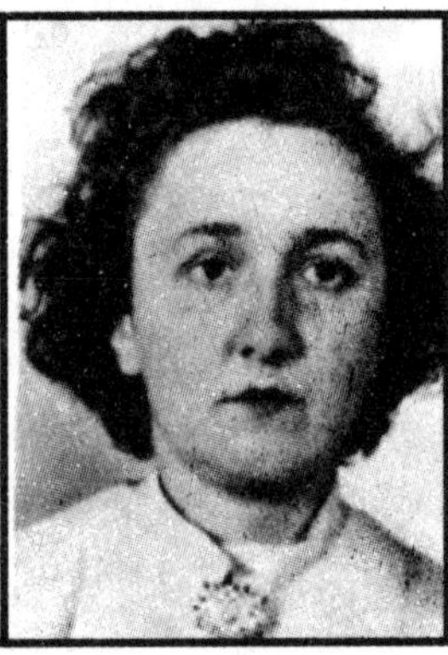

There were three defendants, Julius Rosenberg, his wife Ethel, and their confederate Morton Sobell, who had fled to Mexico but had subsequently been extradited. They were jointly charged with conspiring together with others, including Ethel Rosenberg's brother, David Greenglass; Harry Gold, a Swiss-born Russian, whose real name was Goldnitsky; and Anatoli Yakovlev, a Soviet agent who was ostensibly a clerk in the Soviet Consulate-General in New York.

The object of the alleged conspiracy was a plan to deliver information, documents, sketches, and material vital to the national defence of the United States to a foreign power—namely Soviet Russia—in violation of the Espionage Act of 1917. All these individuals had originally been charged in the Grand Jury indictment.

However, Gold pleaded guilty and was sentenced to 30 years. Greenglass and Yakovlev were ordered to be tried separately, but Greenglass, who had also pleaded guilty, had not yet been sen¬tenced. Yakovlev was not apprehended, since he managed to escape to the Soviet Union before F.B.I. agents could catch up with him.

The Hon. Irving R. Kaufman, one of the district judges for the Southern District of New York, presided on the bench. The prosecution was led by U.S. District Attorney Irving H. Saypol, who had three assistants. The Rosenbergs were defended by Emanuel H. Bloch, a well-known criminal lawyer, and his father Alexander Bloch. O. John Rogge held a watching brief for Greenglass, who was expected to testify for the prosecution.

After the three defendants on trial had pleaded not guilty, the District Attorney opened the case for the prosecution. "The significance of a conspiracy to commit espionage," he said, speaking in deadly earnest tones, "takes on an added meaning here where the defendants are charged with having participated in a conspiracy against our country at the most critical hour in its history, a time of war." He continued: "The evidence will reveal to you how the Rosenbergs persuaded David Greenglass . . . to plot the treacherous role of modern Benedict Arnold while wearing the uniform of the United States Army. We will prove that the Rosenbergs devised and put into operation with the aid of Soviet nationals and Soviet agents in this country an elaborate scheme which enabled them, through Greenglass, to steal the one weapon which might well hold the key to the survival of this nation and the peace of the world—the atomic bomb."

The prosecutor gave due credit to the F.B.I. for breaking the spy ring. At the same time, he made it clear that this could not have been done had it not been for the information revealed by a German-born naturalised British subject named Klaus

Fuchs—who had pleaded guilty in England to spying for the Soviet Union, and received the maximum sentence of 14 years under the relevant British statute.

Fuchs, who was one of the senior scientific officers at the British Atomic Research Establishment at Harwell—had been sent to the United States during the war to cooperate in the development and production of the atomic bomb at Los Alamos. While there he had witnessed the explosion of the first test bomb in New Mexico. Nothing was hidden from him, said J. Edgar Hoover, Director of the F.B.I., "Dr. Fuchs had all our greatest secrets."

After Fuchs began to serve his sentence in England, F.B.I. agents were allowed to question him, and subsequently got on to the trail of the Soviet spy ring in the United States. Fuchs was able to identify Harry Gold, a biochemist whom the Bureau had previously suspected of being active in Soviet espionage, but whom it had previously been impossible to incriminate. The British in turn had picked up Fuchs through the revelations of a Russian cypher clerk named Igor Gouzenko, who was employed in the Military Attache's office in the Soviet Embassy in Ottawa.

The first of the star witnesses to be called to the stand was Max Elitcher, an electronics engineer who had worked in the U.S. Navy Bureau of Ordnance between 1938 and 1948. Elitcher admitted to being a Communist and to having become a member of a "cell" at Sobell's urging. It was also through Sobell that the witness had met the Rosenbergs and learned that they were active party members and secret Soviet agents.

Julius Rosenberg, Elitcher went on, invited him to help transmit secret information from the ordnance office files. Elitcher swore that he pretended to do so, but in fact he had never given Rosenberg any information classified as secret.

Under cross-examination, Elitcher admitted that he lied when he took a loyalty oath. But he firmly insisted that "ever since the F.B.I. got hold of him he had told the entire truth". Finally, Elitcher admitted that he had regularly acted as a courier between Sobell and Rosenberg.

Ruth Greenglass then testified that her husband, David had been a Communist, and described how in the autumn of 1944 Julius Rosenberg had asked her to go to Los Alamos and obtain classified information from David—a member of the United States armed forces and working on an atomic bomb project there. At first she demurred, but Julius assured her that her husband would want to help. Russia was an ally of the U.S., argued Julius, and as such deserved information about the bomb, but Communists were not getting the information which they should. Eventually, said the witness, she agreed to make the trip, as her second wedding anniversary was coming up and she wanted to spend it with her husband. Julius gave her $150 for her expenses, saying the money came from "his friends the Russians".

At first David Greenglass was reluctant to cooperate. The next morning, however, he agreed to give his wife "the general layout of the Los Alamos project", together with the number of employees, the experiments being conducted, and the names of the scientists working there. The witness carefully memorised this information, she said, and duly passed it on to Julius Rosenberg on her return to New York.

In January 1945, she continued, her husband came to New York on leave, and they both met the Rosenbergs by appointment at the latters' apartment. They were introduced to a Mrs. Sidorovich. First, they discussed the kind of information Greenglass should look out for when he returned to Los Alamos. Rosenberg then explained that Mrs. Sidorovich might be sent to New Mexico to get this information from Greenglass, and he produced two torn halves of a Jello box top.

It was arranged that Mrs. Greenglass, who planned to return to New Mexico with her husband should keep one part, and whoever was sent to get in touch with her and her husband would establish his or her identity by producing the other half. Ruth Greenglass remembered that when David commented on the simplicity and cleverness of this device, Julius Rosenberg remarked, "The simplest things are always the cleverest."

Subsequently, contact was made in June 1945, when the Greenglasses were living in Albuquerque, New Mexico. Early one morning, a man called on them. "I come from Julius," he said, and produced the matching piece of the Jello box top. Ruth Greenglass identified him as Harry Gold, who gave her husband $500 which David Greenglass handed over to her.

By May 1950, the witness said, she and her husband, who had then been discharged from the army—were back in New York, and their relations with the Rosenbergs were closer than ever. On May 24, according to Ruth, Julius Rosenberg burst into their apartment brandishing a copy of the *New York Herald Tribune,* which carried a picture of Harry Gold on the front page together with the news of his arrest as a Soviet spy. "You will be next," said Julius, and urged them to escape at once to Mexico.

Ruth did not think their ten-month-old baby could stand the trip. Rosenberg, however, brushed aside her objection and left $1000 with them to cover preliminary expenses, telling her to have passport photographs taken and get vaccinated against smallpox. In spite of these warnings, the Greenglasses stayed in New York. On June 15, David was arrested.

In cross-examination, Alexander Bloch tried to bring out that the witness knew she had committed a crime, and that her direct testimony had been influenced by fear of the F.B.I. "Weren't you frightened of the F. B. I?" he asked.

"Everyone is frightened by the F.B.I.," Ruth Greenglass replied, "but it was not because I realised it was a crime that I was frightened. I didn't think the F.B.I. wanted my husband, I thought they wanted someone my husband would lead them to, someone much more important than he and much more deeply involved."

David Greenglass generally corroborated his wife's testimony when he followed her on the witness stand. However, he denied that he had known of the atomic bomb until he had learned about it from Julius Rosenberg. As a machinist at Los Alamos, he knew only that he was working on "a secret device of some kind".

The details, he insisted, he had first learned from Rosenberg in January 1945 — "fissionable material at one end of a tube and on the other end a sliding mechanism with fissionable material, and when the two were brought together under tremendous pressure nuclear reaction was accomplished." As far as it went, this description fitted the uranium bomb which was dropped on Hiroshima seven months later.

In the following September, he continued, he and his wife went to New York, where he met the Rosenbergs and handed over a sketch of the atom bomb and a ten-page analysis, which Ethel later typed out. "This is very good," said Julius when he read it. "These particulars," said Greenglass, related to the plutonium bomb which was dropped on Nagasaki. The witness's testimony in this respect revealed such an expert knowledge that Judge Kaufman ordered the court to be cleared, and cautioned the newspaper reporters present "to exercise discretion in what they printed".

The tension created in the courtroom by the witness's long recital of treachery was relieved by a small touch of humour at its close. He was asked in cross-examination if, when looking at the Jello box top, he had noticed the flavour.

"Yes raspberry," he promptly replied. This answer raised the only laugh in the sombre proceedings.

Harry Gold was the next prosecution witness. He told how he had been working for the Russians as far back as 1935, and how in 1944 he acted as a go-between for Russian agents and persons who procured information for them. At that time, his Soviet superior was Anatoli Yakovlev, but Gold only knew him as "John". It was at Yakovlev's instruction that in June 1944, the witness first met Fuchs who promised to give him information "relating to the application of nuclear fission to the production of a military weapon".

At a subsequent meeting in Cambridge, Mass., in January 1945, Fuchs told the witness that he was working on the atomic bomb with other scientists in Los Alamos, which he described, particularly mentioning a lens which was one of its essential parts. It was agreed between them that Gold should visit Los Alamos in June—when Fuchs hoped to have more information about the bomb and its lens.

When Gold told Yakovlev of this, the Soviet master spy intimated that he had another very "vital" job for him in New Mexico, namely to contact Greenglass in Albuquerque. At first the witness objected, he said, but when Yakovlev insisted he agreed, since he took this to be an order. After he had seen Fuchs, and obtained a sealed envelope from him, Gold went on to Albuquerque where he met the Greenglasses and received another envelope from them.

A few days later, he reported to Yakovlev in Brooklyn, handing over the two envelopes, which Yakovlev later told him contained "extremely excellent and very valuable" information. The witness's last meeting with Yakovlev took place at the end of 1946, the day before Yakovlev sailed for Europe.

Gold was not cross-examined. This was good tactics on the part of Sobell's attorneys, since Gold's testimony had not implicated their client in any way. As for the Rosenbergs' counsel, they may well have decided not to cross-examine, because Gold had shown himself eager to help the government in any way he could—and answers elicited in cross-examination might only have made matters worse for the Rosenbergs.

Several other witnesses testified to the value of the information imparted by Greenglass as being of "inestimable value to a nation which did not possess the secret of nuclear fission". If Sobell and the Rosenbergs had committed the crimes they were charged with, they said, their actions seriously jeopardised the security of the United States.

Emanuel Bloch opened the defence by calling Julius Rosenberg to the witness stand. Answering his attorney, Rosenberg admitted that he was a first-generation American of Russian parents who had emigrated to New York City. He was a Bachelor of Science, having graduated from New York City College. He told how he married Ethel Greenglass, and in 1940 became a junior engineer in the U.S. Signal Corps, from which he was dismissed five years later.

"Did you ever have any conversation with Ruth Greenglass about November, 1944 with respect to getting information from David Greenglass at the place where he was working?"

"I did not."

"Did you know in the middle of 1944 where David Greenglass was stationed?"

"I did not."

"Did you know in the middle of 1944 that there was such a project known as the Los Alamos project?"

"I did not."

"Did you ever give Ruth Greenglass $ 150, or any other sum for her to go out to visit her husband at Los Alamos for the purpose of trying to enlist him in espionage work?"

"I did not."

Julius Rosenberg denied everything. Shown the sketch of the atomic bomb that David Greenglass had made, he denied that his brother-in-law had ever delivered such a sketch to him. "I never saw this sketch before." Apart from what he had heard in court, he could not describe the bomb. Nor had he ever taken a course in nuclear or advanced physics.

He also denied all knowledge of the Jello box top; he had never introduced David Greenglass to a Mrs. Sidorovich. Nor had he tried to induce the Greenglasses to leave the country, and he had not provided them with money for their trip. Finally, he denied that he and his wife had ever contemplated fleeing from America themselves.

Asked in cross-examination by Saypol whether he had been discharged from his job in the Signals Corp because he was suspected of being a Communist, and thus belonging to an illegal organisation, he admitted that this was so.

"Were you a member of the Communist Party?" the District Attorney asked.

Rosenberg paused for a few moments. Then he replied: "I refuse to answer on the ground that it might tend to incriminate me."

He repeated this reply when confronted with a statement he had signed on joining the Signals Corp stating that he was not then, and never had been, a member of the Communist Party. The court sustained the witness's objection to incriminating questions, and ruled that he was not required to answer them.

At the same time, in answer to further questions, Rosenberg protested his loyalty to the United States. "I will fight for this country if it were engaged in a war with any other country," he declared. On the other hand, he admitted that he felt some admiration for the achievements of the Russians—particularly in improving the lot of the underdog. "I felt and still feel," he added, "that they contributed a major share in destroying the Hitler beast who killed six million of my co-religionists, and I feel emotional about that thing."

Judge Kaufman intervened at this point to ask a couple of questions which the witness tried to dodge.

"Did you approve the Communist system of Russia over the capitalist system of this country?"

"I am not an expert on those things, Your Honour, and I did not make any such statement."

"Did you ever belong to any group that discussed the system of Russia?"

Again the witness took refuge behind the protective constitutional amendment. "Well, Your Honour, I feel at this time that I refuse to answer a question that might tend to incriminate me."

Ethel Rosenberg's testimony was along the same lines. She blandly asserted that she was a loyal citizen of the United States and had never engaged in espionage. Everything her brother and sister-in-law had testified to was false, she said. But when she was asked in cross-examination about her affiliations with the Communist Party, she refused to answer.

No further witnesses were called for the defence, since Morton Sobell did not testify. In rebuttal, the prosecution called a New York commercial photographer, who stated that about mid-June 1950, the Rosenbergs and their two children had three sets of passport photographs taken in his studio. Mr. Rosenberg, the witness said, told him that they were going to France to look at some property Mrs. Rosenberg owned there.

In his closing speech to the jury on behalf of the Rosenbergs, Emanuel Bloch concentrated on the unreliability of Ruth and David Greenglass as witnesses. "Don't you think that the Greenglasses put it over on the government when Ruth Greenglass was not even indicted?" he asked the jurors. She walked out and put Greenglass's sister in. David Greenglass was willing to bury his sister and her husband to save his life. Not only are the Greenglasses self-confessed spies, but they are mercenary spies. "They'd do anything for money."

"Any man who will testify against his own flesh and blood, his own sister, is repulsive, revolting, and is violating any code of civilisation that ever existed. He is lower than the lowest animal I have ever seen.

"The Greenglasses have told the truth," asserted District Attorney Saypol in winding up for the prosecution. "They have tried to make amends for the hurt which has been done to our, nation and to the world."

In reality, the D.A. continued, the unreliable testimony came from the Rosenbergs—who had denied planning to leave the country, in spite of the testimony about the passport photographs. "The Rosenbergs have magnified their treachery by lying here." Furthermore, they were linked with Sobell in their espionage activities—since Sobell had flown to Mexico with his family in the same month that Greenglass had been paid by the Russians, through Rosenberg, to do likewise. "Sobell's conduct fits the pattern of membership in this conspiracy and flight from an American jury when the day of reckoning had come."

After the fairest and most impartial summing up of the evidence by Judge Kaufman, the jury retired at 4.53 in the afternoon of March 28 and did not return until 11 o'clock next morning—when they pronounced all three defendants guilty as charged.

"Your crime is worse than murder," Judge Kaufman told the Rosenbergs when they came up for sentence. "In your case I believe your conduct in putting into the hands of the Russian the A-bomb years before our best scientists predicted Russia would perfect the bomb has already caused the Communist aggression in Korea, with resulting casualties exceeding 50,000 Americans."

While not doubting for a moment that Morton Sobell was also engaged in espionage activities, the judge said he was bound to recognise the lesser degree of his implication. He was consequently given 30 years, the maximum prison term provided by the statute. Next day, David Greenglass was sentenced to 15 years in the light of the considerable help he had rendered in the prosecution of the Rosenbergs.

A series of appeals and petitions followed, which in the case of the Rosenbergs had the effect of delaying the execution of the death sentence for more than two years. Their petition for executive clemency was presented to President Truman on January 11, 1953. It was supported by a flood of letters mostly in favour of the sentence being commuted. Among the writers were Albert Einstein, the world-famous scientist—who had earlier urged President Roosevelt to make sure that the United States did not fall behind in the race to make the atom bomb—and a group of 3000 lawyers who declared that "the death penalty would not conform to the great pattern of Anglo-Saxon jurisprudence". But President Truman declined to act on the petition which reached him during the last days of his term of office, and he left the decision to General Dwight D. Eisenhower, his successor in the White House.

President Eisenhower refused to interfere with the sentence on the Rosenbergs. Meanwhile, the appeals and motions for stays of execution continued. At the beginning of June, the Rosenbergs' counsel announced that their clients had rejected the offer which had been made to them on behalf of the Attorney-General that their sentences would be commuted to life imprisonment if they made full confessions and exposed any other members of their spy ring who had not been brought to justice.

"By asking us to repudiate the truth of our innocence," they said at the time. "The government admits its doubts concerning our guilt. We will not help to purify this foul record of a fraudulent and barbarous sentence." Shortly afterwards the Supreme Court voted by a majority of five to four against granting a further stay of execution.

At the last moment, however, it looked as if there would be a stay when Supreme Court Justice Douglas ordered it in response to an application for time to argue a point of law—namely that the Espionage Act of 1917 had been superseded by the Atomic Energy Act of 1946, under which a death sentence could not be imposed except on the recommendation of a jury. On June 19, Justice Douglas's decision was revoked by a majority of the Supreme Court. Defence counsel submitted a final petition to the President for clemency which Eisenhower again rejected.

The Rosenbergs went to the electric chair in Sing-Sing the same evening and met their end bravely, protesting their innocence to the last. The time of execution was advanced from the usual hour of 11 p.m. to 8 p.m. to avoid carrying out the sentences on the Jewish Sabbath.

Julius and Ethel Rosenberg were the first Americans to be sentenced to death for espionage by a non-military court—while Mrs. Rosenberg was the first woman in the United States since Mrs. Surratt had been sentenced for her part in the assassination of President Lincoln, to suffer death by the judgement of a Federal tribunal.

The Dreyfus Affair

The Dreyfus Affair involved the arrest and conviction in 1895 of French Captain Alfred Dreyfus on charges of treason. The case and the aftermatch caused a division in French military and political circles.

Alfred Dreyfus was born in Alsace, France, the son of a Jewish textile manufacturer. His family eventually moved to Paris where in 1880 he entered École Polytechnique Military School. He would eventually make his way through the military ranks where he rose to the rank of Captain. In 1892, he took the War College examination but was given poor scores from General Boonefond, a member of the panel judging the candidate. Boonefond felt that Jews were not desired on the staff. Dreyfus and another Jewish candidate protested the action, but to no avail.

In 1894, French Army counter-intelligence became aware that military information related to new artillery positions was being passed to the Germans. It was determined that the person passing it must be in a position high up in the General staff. Suspicion fell upon Dreyfus, who was arrested and convicted of treason in a secret court martial, was stripped of his military rank and was sentenced to life imprisonment on Devil's Island in French Guiana.

In 1896, Lieutenant Colonel Georges Picquart presented evidence that showed that Dreyfus was not the party guilty of passing the information, but instead that Major Ferdinand Walsin Esterhazy had done so. The French government sought to silence Picquart by transferring him to southern Tunisia, but the information had been leaked to the French press. Dreyfus case had been championed by Emile Zola, the author of the pamphlet *J'Accuse,* an open letter published on January 13, 1898, in the newspaper *L'Aurore.* Zola pointed out judicial errors as well as how flimsy the evidence was against Dreyfus. He also accused the French government and then-President Felix Faure of anti-semitism. Because of his stance and the stir that he caused, Zola was found guilty of libel in February, 1898 and fled to England. Public outrage over the anti-semetic overtones of the prosecution as well as the following coverup forced the French President, Emile Loubet to grant a pardon Dreyfus in 1899 and he was released from prison. Although he was no longer in prison, he was officially still termed a traitor. He stated that "The government of the Republic has given me back my freedom. It is nothing for me without my honor."

Finally on July 12, 1906, Dreyfus was officially exonerated by a military tribunal and was reinstated in the army, now as a Major. After serving in World War I, he eventually rose to the rank of Lieutenant Colonel and received the Croix de Guerre for his service. Dreyfus died on July 12, 1935 in Paris.

The Guillaume Affair

The Guillaume Affair was an espionage scandal that threatened to bring down the government of West Germany during the Cold War.

Willy Brandt was born Herbert Ernst Karl Frahm to an unwed mother in the Free and Hanseatic City of Lübeck, a part of the German empire. At the age of 19, he fled Germany to escape Nazi persecution and changed his name to Willy Brandt to avoid detection by Nazi agents hunting him down

for his anti-Nazi activities. He soon thereafterbecamea Norwegian citizen. He returned to Germany in 1946 and became the Mayor of Berlin in 1957, a position he would hold until 1966 when he became the German Foreign Minister and Vice-Chancellor. In 1969, he was elected Chancellor of the Federal Republic of Germany.

As Chancellor, Brandt was a controversial but admired figure for his work in trying to solidify relations between West Germany and Cold War adversaries. He was named Time magazine's Man of the Year in 1970 and in 1971 and was awarded the Nobel Peace prize for his work in improving relations between Poland, East Germany and the Soviet Union. He negotiated a peace treaty with Poland and agreed on boundaries between Poland and West Germany as well as between Czechoslovakia and West Germany.

One of Brandt's closest aides was his personal assistant Gunter Guillaume. In 1973, West German intelligence agents became suspicious of Gullaume and determined that he was an East German spy operating under Markus Wolf, the head of intelligence for the East German Ministry for State Security and Guillaume was arrested on April 24, 1974. He was sentenced to 13 years in prison for espionage and his wife Christel was sentenced to eight for aiding him. They had both become spies for the East Germans in 1956 and returned to the country in 1981 as they were released separately in a prisoner exchange between the East and West German governments. Guillaume was treated as a hero upon his return.

For Brandt and his Social Democratic Party, the revelation was an enormous blow to an already fragile government. Brandt had been caught up in several scandals for alleged adultery as well as other personal issues. He accepted the brunt of the blame for Guillaume's espionage and resigned from his position as Chancellor on May 6, 1974.

Despite Brandt's suggestion that Guillaume was planted as a spy in order to orchestrate his (Brandt's downfall) Markus Wolf later swore that such was not the case and that the Guillaume affair had been of the biggest mistakes in the history of the East German secret service.

PERSONALITY DEVELOPMENT

9450 B • Rs. 195/-

5642 A • Rs. 150/-

9447 C • Rs. 88/-
8966 E • Rs. 88/-

9973 E • Rs. 110/-

5639 B • Rs. 75/-

9070 B • Rs. 175/-

8868 D • Rs. 150/-

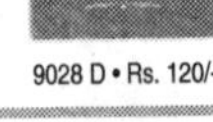

9028 D • Rs. 120/-

9981 B • Rs. 120/-

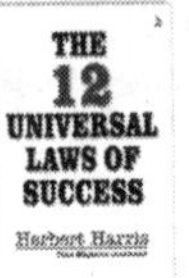

9088 C • Rs. 195/-

8997 B • Rs. 96/-

9430 B • Rs.150/-

COMPUTERS

0000 • Rs. 150/-

7766 A • Rs. 120/-

9460 J

7712 K • Rs. 96/-

7711 J • Rs

STUDENT DEVELOPMENT

9457 E • Rs. 150/-

9455 C • Rs. 150/-

8962 A • Rs. 96/-

4016 D • Rs. 96/-

9089 D • Rs. 135/-

9967 C • Rs. 120/-

9071 D • Rs. 96/-

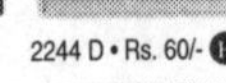

2244 D • Rs. 60/- H

9441 S • Rs. 195/-

5622 A • Rs. 108/-

9090 A • Rs. 160/-

2241 J • Rs. 68/-

PARENTING

8261 D • Rs. 150/-

8919 D • Rs

BODY/BEAUTY CARE

8093 D • Rs. 150/-

9986 B • Rs. 120/-

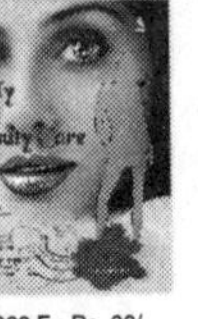

9922 F • Rs. 96/-

8865 F • Rs. 90/-

8971 B • Rs. 96/-

SAYINGS/QUOTATI PROVERBS

8963 B • Rs. 80/-

9953 A

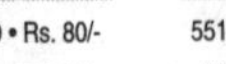

8999 D • Rs. 80/-

5512 A •

9346 C • Rs. 60/-

9425 A

LOVE, SEX & ROMANCE

8260 D • Rs. 96/-

8266 D • Rs. 80/-

8278 C • Rs. 80/-

8916 D • Rs. 68/-

8268 C • Rs. 175/-

SELF-IMPROVEMENT

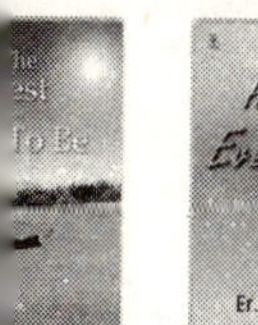
Rs. 195/-

9096 B • Rs. 96/-

4008 J • Rs. 96/- (B)

9027 D • Rs. 120-

8258 D • Rs. 120/-

9026 D • Rs. 175/-

9563 N • Rs. 125/-

Rs. 80/-

9066 B • Rs. 96/-

9081 D • Rs. 96/-

4010 L • Rs. 60/-

9091 B • Rs. 80/-

8885 D • Rs. 68/-

8947 E • Rs. 80/-

Rs. 96/-

8943 C • Rs. 195/-

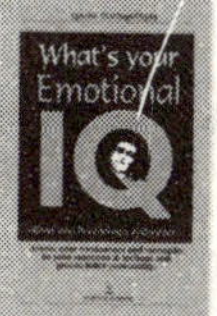

8935 D • Rs. 96/-

8990 C • Rs. 96/-

DIET & NUTRITION

Rs. 96/-

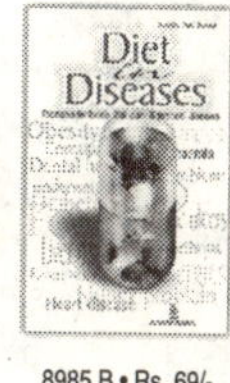
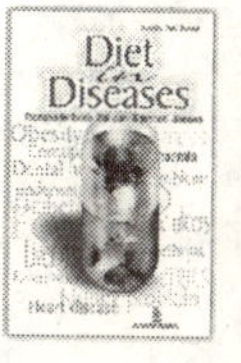

8985 B • Rs. 69/-

8904 D • Rs. 96/-

8276 A • Rs. 80/-

8968 G • Rs. 96/-

RELATIONSHIP

Rs. 72/-

8998 C • Rs. 80/-

9438 B • Rs.150/-

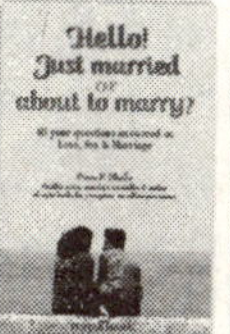

9065 A • Rs. 80/-

9994 E • Rs. 120/-

JOB / CAREER

5623 B • Rs. 195/-

9404 D • Rs. 195/-

9439 C • Rs. 150/-

9431 C • Rs.175/-

4017 D • Rs. 120/-

4018 D • Rs. 80/-

9535 C • Rs. 150/-

ALTERNATIVE THERAPIES

8983 E • Rs. 80/- | 8941 A • Rs. 80/- | 8879 C • Rs. 60/- | 5637 D • Rs. 96/-

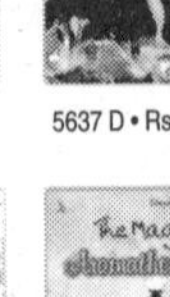

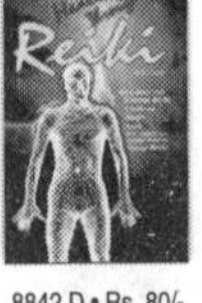

8882 F • Rs. 150/- | 8842 D • Rs. 80/- | 8889 D • Rs. 80/- | 8836 D • Rs. 135/-

8271 C • Rs. 96/- | 2317 E • Rs. 60/- | 9935 F • Rs. 108/- | 9950 B • Rs. 80/-

GENERAL HEALTH

8877 A • Rs. 120/- | 8870 D • Rs. 60/- | 9029 D • Rs. 68/- | 9075 C • Rs. 160/- | 9940 D • Rs. 120/-

8938 D • Rs. 88/- | 8948 A • Rs. 96/- | 9025 D • Rs. 80/- | 9038 D • Rs. 68/- | 8859 G • Rs. 80/-

SLIMMING & FITNESS

9445 A • Rs. 150/- | 8277 B • Rs. 80/- | 8875 K • Rs. 80/- | 8847 M • Rs. 60/-

COMMON AILMENTS & DISEASES

8281 A • Rs. 80/- | 8094 D • Rs. 120/- | 8888 D • Rs. 80/- | 8908 D • R

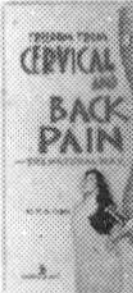

8964 C • Rs. 96/- | 8848 D • Rs. 96/- | 8878 B • Rs. 80/- | 8891 D • F

YOGA & MEDITATION

2118 F • Rs.120/- | 8269 A • Rs.150/- | 9087 B • Rs.96/- | 9998 D • R

9080 C • Rs.24/- | 8939 D • Rs.88/- | 8099 D • Rs.80/- | 8867 D •

8901 D • Rs.120/- | 9958 S • Rs.160/- (with CD) | 2119 G • Rs.96/- | 8892 D • Rs.120/- | 9057 B

HOMEOPATHY

9446 B • Rs.150/- | 8887 D • Rs.175/- | 8270 B •

A • Rs.340/- HB
4128 D • Rs. 250/- Colour (H.B.)
4177 C • Rs. 295/- (H.B.)
9987 E • Rs. 150/-
9585 A • Rs. 96/-
9983 D • Rs. 499/- Colour (H.B.)

3 D • Rs.95/-
4126 B • Rs. 96/-
9505 A • Rs.195/-
4183 A • Rs. 350/- (H.B.)
9514 B • Rs.60/-
4151 A • Rs. 399/- Colour (H.B.)

3 A • Rs. 60/-
8898 D • Rs. 80/-
4124 A • Rs. 80/-
9405 A • Rs. 195/-
4190 C • Rs. 160/-
9984 E • Rs. 399/- Colour (H.B.)

3 A • Rs.175/-
9520 D • Rs. 120/-
9510 B • Rs.120/-
9542 B • Rs. 150/-
4182 D • Rs. 96/-
4130 B • Rs. 120/-
4152 B • Rs. 96/-

B • Rs. 80/-
9509 A • Rs.150/-
9407 C • Rs. 195/-
9525 A • Rs. 150/-
9504 D • Rs.96/-
9989 D • Rs. 96/-
4181 C • Rs. 195/-
9540 D • Rs. 150/-

Commenteries on BHAGAVAD GITA

9 A • Rs. 80/-
4179 A • Rs. 295/- (H.B.)
4132 D • Rs. 80/-
9063 D • Rs. 80/-
9997 C • Rs. 80/-
9959 D • Rs. 80/-
4113 D • Rs. 48/-
4188 A • Rs. 160/-

COOKERY BOOKS

9936 D • Rs. 96/- 9320 A • Rs. 125/- 9297 C • Rs. 125/- 9948 D • Rs. 80/- 9938 D • Rs. 80/-

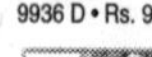

9962 C • Rs. 125/- 9942 D • Rs. 80/- 9944 D • Rs. 80/- 9943 D • Rs. 80/-

MYSTERIES / GHOSTS / ADVENTURE

2331 C • Rs. 60/- 2335 A • Rs. 80/- 9985 A • Rs. 80/- 5164 E • Rs

9977 B • Rs. 96/- 2337 C • Rs. 96/- 2336 B • Rs. 80/- 51107 • Rs

5156 D • Rs. 72/- 5172 F • Rs. 72/- 5121 K • Rs. 72/- 5116 D • Rs

HOMEMAKING / GRILLS & RAILINGS

3111 E • Rs. 175/- 3107 F • Rs. 88/- 3106 E • Rs. 88/- 3108 G • Rs. 90/-

3102 K • Rs. 195/- (H.B.) 3103 L • Rs. 88/- 3104 M • Rs. 88/- 3105 D • Rs. 88/-

JOKES

2319 B • Rs. 96/- 2341 B • Rs. 60/- 2318 A • Rs. 80/- 2330 B • Rs. 80/- 9226 A • R

HUMOUR & SATIRE

2338 D • Rs. 120/- 8890 D • Rs. 68/- 2315 C • Rs. 80/- 2321 D • Rs. 295/- (H.B.) 9340 A • Rs. 96/- 8927 D • Rs. 68/- 2326 E • Rs. 120/-

Moral, Wisdom Fairy Tales

8967 F • Rs. 96/- 9077 E • Rs. 12

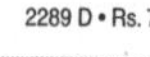

9248 C • Rs. 60/- 2289 D • Rs. 72/

QUIZ BOOKS

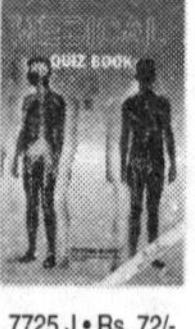

8965 D • Rs. 96/- 7727 L • Rs. 72/- 7723 F • Rs. 72/- 7726 K • Rs. 72/- 7753 G • Rs. 72/- 7722 E • Rs. 72/- 7725 J • Rs. 72/-

• Rs. 175/- 8925 D • Rs. 80/- 8899 D • Rs. 110/- 9432 D • Rs.150/- 8259 D • Rs. 88/- 2125 D • Rs. 80/- 2133 B • Rs. 96/- 2109 F • Rs. 120/- 8902 D • Rs. 80/-

2 A • Rs. 150/- 2127 D • Rs. 150/- 9086 A • Rs. 295/- (HB) 2112 D • Rs. 80/- 2108 E • Rs. 80/- 2116 D • Rs. 110/- 3110 D • Rs. 96/- 2120 D • Rs. 96/-

ENGLISH IMPROVEMENT

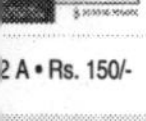
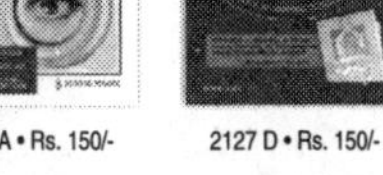

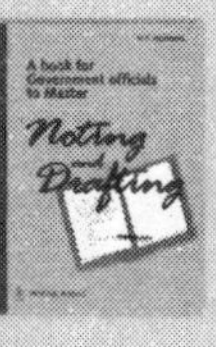

D • Rs. 175/- 5511 E • Rs. 72/- 6651 E • Rs. 175/- 5538 D • Rs. 80/- 6607 L • Rs. 88/- 5541 C • Rs. 196/- 9040 D • Rs. 60/- 9056 A • Rs. 96/-

GENERAL

) • Rs. 80/-HB 9041 A • Rs.195/- 5114 B • Rs.68/- 4175 A • Rs. 195/- 9532 D • Rs. 250/- HB

MAGIC

2250 A • Rs. 110/- 2202 E • Rs. 80/-

2237 M • Rs. 60/- 2242 K • Rs. 60/-

2243 L • Rs. 60/-

FUN, FACTS

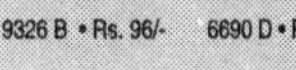

F • Rs. 60/- 9326 B • Rs. 96/- 6690 D • Rs. 60/- 2328 G • Rs. 50/- 2327 F • Rs. 50/- 2211 F • Rs. 60/- 5110 A • Rs. 80/-

MANAGEMENT / BUSINESS & PROFESSION / STOCK MARKET

9461 K • Rs. 135/-

5638 A • Rs. 110/-

8979 A • Rs. 96/-

9406 B • Rs. 150/-

5646 A • Rs. 225/-

5643 B • Rs. 120/-

8972 C • Rs. 80/-

9402 B • Rs. 195/-

5614 E • Rs. 150/-

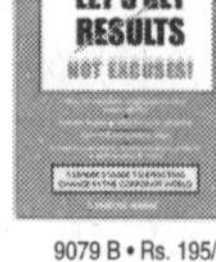
9079 B • Rs. 195/-

9403 C • Rs. 195/-

5618 D • Rs. 88/-

4001 A • Rs. 150/-

4004 D • Rs. 88/-

5641 D • Rs. 195/- (H.B.)

5615 D • Rs. 150/-

5640 C • Rs. 120/-

9313 D • Rs. 150/-

8883 D • Rs. 120/-

4005 E • Rs. 96/-

AYURVEDA

8923 D • Rs. 150/-

8010 D • Rs. 88/-

8944 D • Rs. 175/-

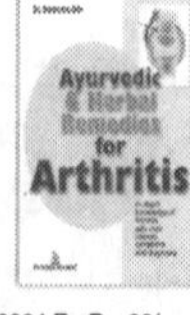
9094 E • Rs. 96/-

FICTION from Cedar books

9459 H • Rs. 1000/-

9587 C • Rs. 125/-

9582 T • Rs. 150/-

9532 D • Rs.

9526 B • Rs. 125/-

9592 H • Rs. 150/-

9512 D • Rs. 250/-

9501 A • R

9530 B • Rs. 175/-

9560 J • Rs. 175/-

9544 D • Rs. 95/-

9522B • Rs

- Fate, Fraud & A Friday Wedding 150.00
- The Ultimate Laugh 150.00
- Cricket Till I Die! 150.00
- Delayed Mansoon 150.00
- What Happened to That Love 125.00
- Did you see The Joker? 125.00
- Luv U Mate 125.00
- Kalika 175.00
- Love was never Mine 150.00
- The K-Word 150.00
- Temple of Destiny 175.00
- The Adventure of the Bubblegum Boy 150.00
- Truly, Madly, Deeply 175.00
- The Long Road 150.00
- The Unheards 150.00
- To catch a Butterfly 95.00
- It can't be you... 175.00
- Far From Normal 150.00
- Somewhere@nowhere 150.00
- Deceivers 150.00
- Some of the Whole 199.00
- Love on Velocity Express 125.00
- A River on fire 95.00
- A Nameless Place 125.00
- Incredible High 175.00
- One Day 125.00
- Fallen Leaf, Withered Wind 15
- Foot Print in The Bajra 17
- Haunting Silhouettes 17
- How I got my Girl Back 15
- Interpretation 12
- The Red Corridor 15
- The God who failed! 9
- Prisoners of Hate 19
- The Wheel Turned 17
- Beyond Diamond Rings 17
- Mask in the Mirror 29
- Dance O' Peacock 17
- Enemy in the Ranks 19
- Friendship@ facebook.com 17
- Vinculum 9
- Dancing on the notes of life 19
- Illusions of Love 19
- Kite Strings 17
- Knots and No Crosses 17
- Men as they are! 12
- Not for $ Anymore 15
- Three Shades of Green 19
- The Angel of God 19
- The Journey of Om 17
- The Second Hand 17
- Under the rain tree 9

PUSTAK MAHAL™
Delhi • Mumbai • Patna • Hyderabad • Bengaluru

J-3/16, Daryaganj (Opp. Happy School) New Delhi-110002
Tel.:23272783-84 • E-mail:orders@pustakmahal.com

For buying online visit our website: www.pustakmahal.com